Verified
Near-Death Experiences

Verified
Near-Death Experiences

Simon Bown

FIRST EDITION
LONDON 2025
Copyright © 2025 Simon Bown

First published in 2025 by Simon G Bown.

The right of Simon G Bown to be identified as the author of this work has been asserted by him in accordance with the Copyright, Designs, and Patents Act 1988.

ALL RIGHTS RESERVED.

No part of this publication may be reproduced, stored in a retrieval system, or transmitted, in any form or by any means, without the prior written permission of the publisher, nor be otherwise circulated in any form of binding or cover other than that in which it is published and without a similar condition including this condition being imposed on the subsequent purchaser.

Simon Bown is the host of

Our Paranormal Afterlife podcast

Alien UFO Podcast

https://www.pastliveshypnosis.co.uk/

Email: si.bown@gmail.com

Layout & Proofreading by:
AJ Parr/Grapevine Books

About the Author

Simon Bown is the host of two influential podcasts, a clinical hypnotherapist, and an author specializing in topics related to consciousness, reincarnation, and the afterlife.

He has produced over 800 podcast episodes, engaging with leading experts and scholars in the fields of Near-Death Experiences (NDEs), reincarnation, and contact with intelligent extraterrestrials. His podcasts, *Alien UFO Podcast*, and *Our Paranormal Afterlife*, have collectively garnered over 6,000,000 downloads, with *Our Paranormal Afterlife* reaching No.1 on the UK Apple Podcasts spirituality chart.

Simon holds a diploma in Clinical Hypnotherapy and is certified in Past Life Regression Therapy. He has conducted hundreds of past life regression sessions, specializing in guiding individuals through these therapeutic processes.

His research is informed by personal experiences with paranormal phenomena, including psychic flashes, UFO sightings, and other unexplained occurrences. These experiences have contributed to his academic interest in the nature of consciousness and its potential existence beyond the physical body.

In addition to his work in podcasting and hypnotherapy, Simon is an avid bass guitarist and science fiction writer.

Note from the Author

Many of the people featured in this book have shared their stories as guests on my podcast, *Our Paranormal Afterlife*. I've had the unique opportunity to speak with them personally, exploring their experiences and the extraordinary events that validate their accounts.

When this book was in its final stages, I shared the chapters with the experiencers to ensure accuracy. Any errors were corrected to keep the information as reliable as possible.

Simon Bown

For Sarah, Izzy, and Emma

My great appreciation and thanks go to,

Barbara Bartolome
Vincent Tolman
Randy Schiefer
Franco Romero
Malcolm Nair
Jeff Olsen
Jeff O'Driscoll
Deborah King
Lynda Cramer
Ryan McCully
Amber Cavanagh
David Wallace
Andrew Elkan
Crystal Faith
Ingrid Honkala
Stephanie Arnold
Jan Holden
AJ Parr

Foreword

The pages you're about to read explore one of the world's most fascinating and mysterious topics: verified near-death experiences. These aren't just stories of strange visions by people who have experienced clinical death or have come close to it—they're accounts from experiencers who say they left their bodies, witnessed events, overheard conversations, or visited the other side and encountered deceased people they couldn't have possibly known about. Some even describe meeting ancestors they had never met before, only to later recognize them in old photographs or through family stories they'd never heard.

While researchers like Dr. Raymond Moody, Dr. Kenneth Ring, Dr. Melvin Morse, Dr. PMH Atwater, and Dr. Jeffrey Long have studied many of such cases for decades, this is the first book I've come across that focuses entirely on verified experiences—those where the details can be confirmed by real-world evidence. That's what makes this book so important.

Written by Simon Bown, a British clinical hypnotherapist and podcaster, this book brings fresh insight into these incredible stories. Simon has spent years researching the afterlife, reincarnation, and consciousness, and what really sets these pages apart is his connection with many of the experiencers featured here. Many have been guests on his popular podcast, *Our Paranormal*

Afterlife, where he's also interviewed top experts in near-death studies and afterlife research. This has allowed him to offer a unique mix of personal stories and expert analysis that's both relatable and eye-opening.

What makes this book especially powerful is how it challenges the widespread idea that NDEs are just hallucinations or random brain activity—still supported by many materialistic scientists. And although the stories shared here raise tough questions about what really happens when we die, they strongly suggest that consciousness actually survives beyond physical death.

Although science doesn't yet have a solid and clear explanation for these events, the growing number of verified cases around the world—many of which are shared in this book—show that this phenomenon deserves serious attention. These accounts hint that death might not be the end after all but rather a transition as well as a new beginning.

In the end, this isn't just a collection of incredible stories—it's a book that will certainly change the way you think about life, death, and what comes next. Whether you're a skeptic, a believer, or just curious, the journey you're about to embark on is definitely bound to blow your mind!

AJ Parr

NDE researcher and best-selling author

Contents

About the Author V
Note from the Author VI
Foreword IX
1. Veridical Near-Death Experiences 1
2. The Peace Above, The Chaos Below 7
3. The Basket, the Web, and the Sister I Never Knew 17
4. Ancestral Guardian: The Mystery of Drake 35
5. The Socks That Confirmed Eternity 53
6. Lost in the City of Eternity 65
7. The Question That Changed Everything 81
8. A Soul's Surrender and a Life Reclaimed 89
9. To What Degree Have You Loved? 99
10. Corinna's Warning: A Life Unfinished 113
11. The Library of Lives 127
12. The Multicolored Tunnel and the Angel Named Elizabeth 139
13. From the Spider's Sting to the Ocean of Souls 147
14. The Garden of What Is and What Could Be 155
15. Standstill Between Two Worlds 169
16. The Guardian and the Waiting Room of Souls 183
17. A Sleeper Who Saw Everything 191
18. The Surgeon's Dance and the Light Beyond 197
19. Three Souls I Would Know 203

20. City of Light and Desert of Shadows............................221

21. The Maid, the Mother, and the Message.......................237

22. Premonition and Proof: A Mother's Brush with the Beyond 245

23. Early 20th-Century Near-Death Experiences................255

24. Dr. Rudy's Christmas Day Case 267

"I once talked to a man who apparently died at birth but was resuscitated," Dr. Raymond Moody explained. *"He told his parents at an early age that he remembered this event. Now, he was very young when he started talking about it and vividly described to them the walls of the room where he was born as being pink. Of course, when they heard this, they thought the boy was making it up."*

Over and over, the kid kept telling his parents about this event, but they always thought it was a childhood fantasy. However, as he grew older, his insistence on the pink walls perplexed them. They were both in the Air Force, and he had been born on a military base in the Philippines, so one day, his father decided to get to the bottom of this puzzling detail and investigate further. In fact, he contacted the hospital where his son was born and managed to get in touch with the doctor who had delivered him. To his astonishment, the doctor confirmed that the operating room had indeed been painted pink at the time of the birth:

This was not by design but out of necessity—the hospital had run out of other colors, and pink was the only paint available. This revelation left his parents speechless and profoundly moved. They realized that their son's recollection was not a fantasy but a genuine memory from his brief brush with death.

"When I heard this story, I was deeply moved and amazed by the intricate details that children could remember from their near-death experiences. It also made me reflect on the nature of such experiences and the profound impact they have on individuals, even from the very start of their lives. The fact that this man could recall such specific details from his birth, which were later verified, was both astounding and humbling."

—AJ Parr, *The Girl Who Visited Heaven and Other Children's Near-Death Experiences*

1. Veridical Near-Death Experiences

"Veridical" is derived from the Latin *veridicus*, meaning "speaking the truth" or "truthful."

"The brain isn't functioning. It's not there. It's destroyed. It's abnormal. But, yet, it can produce these very clear experiences. An unconscious state is when the brain ceases to function. For example, if you faint, you fall to the floor, you don't know what's happening, and the brain isn't working. The memory systems are particularly sensitive to unconsciousness. So you won't remember anything. But yet, after one of these experiences (an NDE), you come out with clear, lucid memories. This is a real puzzle for science. I have not yet seen any good scientific explanation which can explain that fact."

– Dr. Peter Fenwick, Consultant Neuropsychologist, King's College, London

*

Near-death experiences (NDEs) have fascinated both scientists and the general population for decades. Stories of people who have been declared clinically dead or were on the brink of death—only to return with vivid memories of spiritual experiences—have been documented across cultures and throughout history. These experiences are often characterized by vivid sensory perceptions, encounters with spiritual beings, out-of-body experiences (OBEs), and a sense of profound peace and love.

VERIDICAL NEAR-DEATH EXPERIENCES

While NDEs have been the subject of much speculation and study, a particular subset—known as 'veridical near-death experiences'—offers one of the most compelling lines of evidence for the possibility that consciousness can exist independently of the brain.

A veridical NDE refers to a case in which a person gains accurate, verifiable knowledge about events or details they should not have been able to perceive under normal circumstances—especially given their critical physical state. These cases are remarkable because they challenge traditional scientific paradigms that regard consciousness as solely a byproduct of brain activity. They suggest that human awareness might extend beyond the confines of the body, continuing to perceive reality even when brain activity has ceased.

In many cases, people who are in a deep coma, cardiac arrest, or otherwise incapable of sensory perception report witnessing events or conversations that occurred during their unconscious state. This includes detailed observations of hospital rooms, medical staff, or even locations far removed from their physical body. The experiencer often perceives themselves as floating outside their body—usually above it—and experiencing an altered but heightened sense of awareness. After the experiencer recovers, the details they provide are confirmed by witnesses or other forms of evidence. This verification is critical to defining an NDE as "veridical."

*

The "Maria's Shoe" Case

One of the most famous veridical NDEs is the case of "Maria," a woman in Seattle who suffered a heart attack. After being resuscitated, she described an out-of-body experience during which she floated outside the hospital and spotted a blue tennis shoe on a ledge on the third floor. She provided a detailed description—its worn-out condition, a scuff mark on one side, and the way it was positioned just out of sight from anyone below.

A hospital social worker named Kimberly Clark investigated and found the shoe exactly as Maria had described it, perched on a ledge far from her hospital room and completely hidden from both ground-level views and nearby windows. Since Maria had been unconscious, she could not have known about the shoe by any ordinary means.

*

Veridical NDEs have sparked considerable debate in both scientific and philosophical circles. For those with a materialist perspective, these experiences present a significant challenge. If consciousness truly arises from the brain, how can individuals in a state of deep unconsciousness or even clinical death report detailed, accurate knowledge about their surroundings or events that took place far away?

Some neuroscientists argue that veridical NDEs can be explained by the brain's ability to generate vivid experiences during extreme stress. They suggest that the brain might create a last "burst" of consciousness during cardiac arrest or near-death situations. According to this view, the brain may retain and process residual information from the environment, even when seemingly shut down.

However, critics argue that this theory fails to account for the verifiable, specific details that individuals perceive during these experiences. In cases like Maria's shoe, the knowledge gained is far too precise and external to be explained by residual brain activity or hallucinations.

Proposed explanations include:

Quantum Consciousness, where consciousness may not be confined to the brain but instead may operate on a quantum level, allowing it to persist even when brain function ceases. This controversial hypothesis has gained some traction in the study of NDEs.

The theory of Non-local Consciousness suggests that consciousness may exist independently of the brain and is capable of interacting with physical reality in ways we do not yet understand. The idea is that the brain acts more like a receiver of consciousness rather than its generator.

The Survival Hypothesis posits that consciousness can survive bodily death and that veridical NDEs are glimpses of this post-mortem state.

The idea that consciousness might survive physical death aligns with philosophical dualism, the notion that the mind and body are separate entities. Dualists argue that the mind or soul could continue to exist after the body dies, and veridical NDEs provide potential evidence for this view. These experiences suggest that the self, or conscious awareness, might not be entirely tied to the physical brain and could continue beyond death.

If veridical NDEs are genuine, their implications are profound and could reshape our understanding of life and death, potentially reducing the fear of death and altering medical practices surrounding end-of-life care. Many who have had NDEs report profound transformations in their lives afterward, including a greater sense of purpose, compassion, and decreased fear of death. Veridical NDEs remind us that even in the face of death, the mysteries of human consciousness and the nature of reality may extend far beyond what we currently understand.

2. The Peace Above, The Chaos Below

BARBARA BARTOLOME

He asked, "What did you feel like? What did you see?" Barbara continued, "He completely validated it for himself and all the people in the room. I think that freaked them out."

*

In 1987, at 31, Barbara Bartolome lived in Santa Barbara with her husband and two young children—an eight-year-old son and a five-month-old daughter. A few weeks after giving birth to her daughter, Barbara ruptured a disc in her lower back while lifting a heavy object. Her doctor said the injury was permanent and would confine her to a wheelchair for the rest of her life. Barbara sought a second opinion from a neurosurgeon at St. Francis Hospital in Santa Barbara, who assured her he could repair the injury and help her regain her mobility.

The neurosurgeon scheduled Barbara for a laminectomy discectomy, a procedure to remove fragments from her shattered disc. He also brought an orthopedic surgeon onto the team for added expertise. The neurosurgeon informed Barbara that they would conduct a test the night before surgery to determine whether any disc fragments had pierced her spinal cord, as they were concerned about a potential spinal fluid leak. After checking into the hospital, the staff sent Barbara to the X-ray unit for a myelogram.

In this procedure, the doctors would inject iodine dye into Barbara's spinal cord at the base of her neck. The medical staff instructed her to remain perfectly still on the X-ray table as any movement could cause severe headaches lasting for months. The neurosurgeon and orthopedic surgeon joined the X-ray team in the room to observe the procedure, knowing there wouldn't be enough time to receive the myelogram results before Barbara's surgery scheduled for 7 a.m. the next day. The team included two surgeons, two X-ray technicians, and a nurse. Barbara lay on the table as an X-ray technician beside her pressed a button to tilt the table, gradually moving her into an upright position. This movement would allow the dye to flow downward along her spinal cord. Meanwhile, the other technician sat at a monitor, ready to capture images as the dye moved through her spinal cord to detect any leakage.

As the table began moving, Barbara immediately felt disoriented. "I thought, I wonder if I'm supposed to feel like this? But the two X-ray techs were talking to each other, and I didn't want to interrupt them. As the table kept tilting, I felt weirder and weirder, almost like I was going to faint," Barbara recalled. She wanted to speak up and let them know how she felt, but she found herself unable to say anything or even move.

The cause of the issue became clear: the technician hadn't noticed his finger pressing the wrong button. Instead of raising the table to bring her upright, he was inadvertently lowering her head. The dye injected at the base of Barbara's skull began flowing into her brain, altering the pressure and impairing her brain function. After about three minutes, she started hyperventilating. This finally drew the attention of the technician, who looked up to see her eyes rolled back into her head. "He leaned back to see where his thumb was. And then he had this look of, you know, absolute scared and shock, and 'Oh no, oh my god,'" Barbara recalled.

At that moment, Barbara closed her eyes briefly, and when she opened them, she found herself looking down at the room from above. "I didn't look to see if I had a body. But I felt there was something that the back of my head was against, like the ceiling. I was looking straight down at the top of everyone's heads and the top of the equipment. I had been panicking in my body and feeling very scared because I was hyperventilating. But when I got up on the ceiling, the next second, I was absolutely calm, and it was completely peaceful." From her viewpoint on the ceiling, Barbara watched as one of the team members urgently called a code blue. As she took in the scene, she saw her own body lying below and realized she must have died.

Almost immediately, she sensed a boundless presence beside her. "It felt so incredibly immense," she said. "So knowing of who I was, so connected to me, from the first point of eternity, all the way to the future, throughout eternity.

I literally felt this presence, and it seemed to me that's who God was." Their communication was purely telepathic, an exchange that didn't need words. It was a seamless connection, direct, thoughtful, and deeply intuitive. Barbara understood something important, and said to the presence, "I would really like to go back. If I leave my children in this way, at this time, they won't grow up to be the human beings that they could be if I contribute to them." She also realized she had a life purpose, something she was meant to achieve but hadn't completed yet and she told the presence of her desire to return.

The medical team sprang into action. The two X-ray technicians immediately began performing CPR while a nurse urgently called for a defibrillator. From Barbara's perspective above, she could see the nurse shouting "stat," her panic unmistakable. The intensity of the noise and commotion below upset Barbara. "I felt it was obnoxious. It literally felt very loud, very chaotic. It felt awful. Actually, all the stuff down below was awful compared to what I was experiencing with this being and the sensitive, gentle, kind, and loving nature I was feeling from this being," she said.

A woman entered the room with an oxygen cart and placed a mask over Barbara's face. Moments later, a man arrived carrying a small box. He removed several small white pads, peeling off their backing and carefully pressing them onto various spots on Barbara's chest. Curious, Barbara turned to the presence beside her and asked what the man was doing. Instantly, she felt herself transported from her viewpoint near the ceiling down to the box, now so close she could examine its details as though it were inches from her eyes.

"When I asked that question, I was moved from the ceiling vantage point above my body, right down in front of the box that was on a ledge next to my body that was lying on the X-ray table; there was a ledge and this box was there. I was right in front of the box as if it was like five inches from my eyes. There was a glass area of it and it was greenish," Barbara recalled. The man flipped a toggle switch on the box, illuminating its green screen. A steady monotone sound emitted as a flat green line traced across, showing Barbara's heart had stopped. The moment she saw this, her perspective shifted back up to the ceiling.

Below, the two surgeons discussed the situation. They agreed that too much time was passing and the risk of brain damage was increasing. The lack of a defibrillator heightened the urgency. At last, the orthopedic surgeon directed the two X-ray technicians to step back. Barbara described what happened next. "He stepped two steps forward, took his fist from behind his back, arched it from behind his back over his head, and pounded the center of my body on the X-ray table right where my chest is. When he did that, I watched my body react to the blow, but I did not return to it."

The presence asked her, "But if you go back, you will still be in your marriage. What will you do?" Scenes from her past surfaced, memories from her marriage. Her husband was an angry man, often directing his frustration toward both her and their children. For years, she had gone to great lengths to keep his temper at bay, conforming to his demands to avoid conflict, living in a state of constant vigilance.

The presence presented her with a choice: to return to her body or to move forward into the afterlife. "After I saw those brief film clips of all that stuff, I felt that I had all the time that I needed to make a decision of whether I wanted to stay or whether I wanted to come back. So, I evaluated my relationship with my husband. I realized that it wasn't him that needed to change. It was me. I needed to stop accepting his behaviors. I needed to get out. I needed to get away. I said to God, if you let me go back, I promise you, I'll get strong enough to leave him. The second I said the word 'him,' the doctor did the second precordial thump and restarted my heart."

Barbara suddenly found herself back in her body, and the orthopedic surgeon looked down at her in shock. Barbara said into the oxygen mask, "What just happened?" The nurse quickly intervened, "Stop! Don't talk! We need to stabilize you!"

For the next twenty minutes, the medical team worked to stabilize her condition. Once they removed the oxygen mask, Barbara told them she'd been up by the ceiling, watching everything that had taken place. The neurosurgeon, standing beside her bed, responded with a sarcastic "Oh, brother," as if dismissing her experience entirely.

Barbara described the entire sequence of events she had witnessed from above, recounting every detail with striking accuracy. "I just blurted out everything that had just unfolded down below. She was the person who brought in the oxygen cart and put it on my face. That man brought in a heart monitor. I watched it flatlining. I could hear it making that monotone sound. That one was on the phone the whole time, and she was calling for the defibrillator unit, but it never came in. He was doing CPR with you. One guy was blowing in my mouth, one guy was doing chest compressions. They switched places about every two minutes. I watched that until you said this to him. I told the doctors what they had said in their conversation, and I said, then you stepped forward and struck my chest twice. I completely validated my entire NDE."

She described the neurosurgeon's reaction as she recounted the events. "I watched him. His hands were clenched, and they started shaking, actually started shaking and he had fists clenched, and then he had his teeth kind of clenched. Then, when I stopped, he said, 'I'm not going to stand here and listen to this,' and he stormed out of the room."

The orthopedic surgeon, who has been in contact with Barbara since the incident, held her hand and asked her to recount everything she had witnessed once more. He asked, "What did you feel like? What did you see?" Barbara continued, "he completely validated it for himself and all the people in the room. I think that freaked them out, the rest of the people in the room, you know, the guy who brought in the heart monitor, the lady who brought in the oxygen cart, the nurse that was in there originally, the two X-ray techs, and the orthopedic surgeon, all of them stayed in the room as I continued to validate it. Nobody laughed, and nobody freaked out. Only the neurosurgeon freaked out."

The hospital staff knew well that a procedural error, a mistake made by the man responsible for operating the controls on the table, had caused Barbara's heart to stop. They recognized that this mistake had put Barbara's life in jeopardy, making the incident a potential liability for the hospital. "Not a single person in the hospital would talk to me about it," Barbara recalled. "No one would mention it. They would either look at my chart and say, I don't see anything about that in here. Or they would say, I don't know what you're talking about. I'm sorry."

Verification Events

CPR

Barbara detailed every moment that occurred while she was undergoing CPR, describing actions, sounds, and conversations with startling precision. According to the heart monitor, her heart had completely stopped, and, medically, within 20 seconds of her heart stopping, her brain would have flatlined as well, rendering her physically incapable of perceiving anything through her senses.

She described how a nurse had urgently called for the defibrillator, using the term "STAT." She correctly identified the nurse who brought in the oxygen cart and the man responsible for bringing the heart monitor. She pointed out the two men performing CPR on her, detailing how they alternated between giving her breaths and performing chest compressions, switching roles every two minutes. Her descriptions were precise, noting, "They were blowing in my mouth, but then they just switched and did chest compressions every two minutes and change."

Conversations

Beyond actions, Barbara recounted the conversations people in the room were having, accurately recalling snippets of dialogue and the expressions of concern on their faces. The level of detail in her account left no doubt that she had witnessed the full scene, something that should have been impossible given her physical state. Her descriptions left the medical team both stunned and unsettled, as Barbara's awareness seemed to defy the limits of her physical senses.

3. The Basket, the Web, and the Sister I Never Knew

DEBORAH KING

She asked her daughter, "Who brought that wonderful basket that you were using in the waiting room?" Her daughter asked, "Who told you about that?" Deborah replied, "Well, I saw you, and I described what was in it."

*

Deborah King, PhD, had a life-changing near-death experience in December 2008. From a young age, Deborah felt deeply connected to the spiritual realm and showed strong intuitive abilities. In the years before this event, she had several spiritually transformative experiences. However, these often clashed with her Catholic upbringing.

At 17 years old, in January 1972, Deborah took a day off school to focus on preparing for college. During the day, she joined her father on a quick trip, riding in the front passenger seat of their car. They came to a stop at a red light, and after it turned green they moved forward. Out of nowhere, a drunk truck driver ran his red light, hitting the passenger-side door where Deborah was sitting causing the car to roll over multiple times.

In an instant, Deborah found herself outside her body, hovering above the scene of the accident. Looking down, she could see the mangled remains of the car. The impact had thrown her body into the back seat, and the front passenger door, where she had been sitting moments before, was a twisted, almost flattened mass of metal. Her father had minor injuries and quickly got out of the car. As he ran around the wreck, he held his head and throat. Deborah watched as he desperately tried to wake her. Although she had no concern for herself, she was worried about her father and wanted to tell him she was safe. The rescue services arrived, and Deborah quickly returned to her body. "I remember opening my eyes and feeling glass on my face, and I was aware that I was bleeding," she recalled. "I had multiple injuries. I was in a lot of pain. Then I heard my father's voice saying, 'Thank God, thank God, Debbie, you're going to be okay.'"

While Deborah was in hospital recovering, her father didn't talk about his own injuries. It wasn't until her mother told her he had a serious neck injury that Deborah found what had happened to him. The damage was due to the shoulder harness in their 1970s car exerting too much pressure during the sudden impact. This helped explain something Deborah had seen during her out-of-body experience. While hovering above the accident, she had clearly seen her father clutching his head and throat.

Deborah told no one about her experience. She was afraid to talk about it because she didn't fully understand how it happened herself and didn't want to be seen as strange or 'just imagining things,' especially as she was about to start her education in healthcare.

After college, Deborah moved to Maryland, where she started her career in medicine. In 1977, Deborah was working as an intensive care nurse at Johns Hopkins. At the end of a long and very tiring evening shift, a patient in his 40s was admitted to the intensive care unit from the emergency room. While conducting the initial assessment of injuries, the patient unexpectedly went into cardiac arrest. The team immediately started resuscitation, administering drugs, oxygen and intubating him. Despite an enormous amount of effort, the patient was not responding, and they couldn't get a consistent heartbeat.

As time passed, Deborah saw the medical team becoming increasingly discouraged, and there was a growing sense of doubt the man would survive. The chief resident decided they were not making progress and should call the time of death. "But when he said that, a feeling came over me," Deborah recalled. "The only way I can describe it is an intuitive knowing that we needed to keep going. That somehow, if we just kept going, we would get him back." Acting on this intuitive feeling, which she did not fully understand herself, Deborah asked the chief resident to go "one more round." He agreed, although she got the feeling that he had little faith it would work, and that, as the nurse in charge that evening, he was agreeing more as a gesture of teamwork than anything else. After this last round of effort, to everyone's surprise, the patient's heart regained a viable rhythm and his other parameters stabilized. There was a great sense of relief in the team, but despite this success, they were concerned, as the patient was not waking up. They put him on a ventilator and gave him medication, hoping he would regain consciousness.

Two days later, Deborah returned to the hospital to start a shift and visited the patient. "I walked into the patient's room, and the second he saw me, before I said anything, he leaned forward in the bed and kind of pulled his oxygen mask away from his face and said, 'It's you, you're the one.' He pointed to the ceiling of the ICU room and said, 'I was up there. I was watching the whole thing. I saw everything. I saw the lead resident with blood on his shirt, and you were conversing with him.'" The resident had been working on a trauma resuscitation in the emergency room before coming to work with Deborah and did have blood on his clothing. He continued to describe Deborah's long hair correctly, noting that it fell forward, that she looked very tired, and told her exactly where she was standing. He described the problems the team had trying to place his endotracheal tube.

He accurately described the anesthesiologist who assisted as a tall man with glasses, a blue hat, and blue scrubs. "I was thinking, how could this person who was in a complete cardiac arrest know these things?" Deborah recalled. During his resuscitation, the patient had had a flat line on the EKG monitor. His brain was in no condition to make and retain complex memories. "He had no blood pressure, no pulse. There was no profusion to his brain, and therefore, accessing what I know of science, he could not have a conscious experience," she explained. "His brain was not working."

Deborah was stunned when the patient said he heard her clearly say to the resident, "Let's go one more round," she recalled. "He said, 'Thank you. Thank you, nurse, for saying that.' I just remember getting covered with chills from my head to my toes. I just really didn't know what to say, but I knew that everything he was telling me was true." She remembered her own experience during her car accident when she could see everything from above the scene. But she didn't perceive the same level of detail this patient described in his experience. Also, when she had her out-of-body experience, she wasn't in full cardiac arrest as this patient had been.

She told no one about what had happened, again fearing that her colleagues would judge her negatively, concerned about the impact this might have on her professional practice. She earned a master's degree in nursing and a doctoral degree in clinical psychology. She then moved from acute care to work in home care and hospice, and later started her career as a psychotherapist specializing in behavioural medicine.

In 2008, at age 54, Deborah had a powerful Near-Death Experience that was much more detailed and 'deep' than the out-of-body experience she had during her car accident many years before. It had been six months since her father passed away, and she had driven the five-hour round trip to visit his grave. When she returned home, her husband, Bob, greeted her and told her he was very relieved that she had arrived home okay, saying that she looked very tired. As she was exhausted, she went to bed to read a book. Bob later told her he had a strong intuitive feeling that she was not okay and that he should stay with her. As Deborah sat reading her book, she suddenly straightened and placed her hands on her head. Alarmed, she said, "Oh my God, Bob, I am so dizzy. I'm just so incredibly dizzy." Bob watched in shock as she slumped forward, unresponsive.

Realizing she wasn't breathing, he quickly checked for a pulse but found none. Fortunately, Deborah had taught Bob CPR and he immediately began resuscitation efforts while calling 911. He performed chest compressions and rescue breaths, fighting to keep her alive until paramedics arrived. When the emergency team took over, Bob stood by as they administered defibrillations. After a number of attempts, they found a pulse and connected an IV. Several times during the trip to the hospital, her heart lost a viable rhythm. After they had arrived, a doctor told Bob he didn't think she was going to survive, but if she did, there was a clear risk she would have some degree of brain damage.

Deborah's body went into Decerebrate Posturing. This unusual body position occurs automatically when the brain has suffered significant, often permanent, damage and is often considered a grim sign, as many patients with decerebrate posturing do not survive. Two doctors discussed Deborah's condition with Bob and recommended a new protocol called Therapeutic Hypothermia. The plan was to lower her body temperature to protect her brain from damage. After transferring Deborah to the intensive care unit, the medical team stabilized her. However, she had fallen into a coma.

"I really can't tell you when my NDE began," she recalled. "In the middle of my cardiac arrest? My resuscitation? My coma? I can just tell you that the first thing I remember was being in what I would call a black void." This vast, timeless expanse seemed to be a holding place, and a sense of comfort enveloped her. Deep within, she knew she wouldn't stay there for long. Then, a realization dawned upon her: she was dead. Being a nurse, she performed a body assessment to confirm her suspicions. "I was like, Okay, no arms, no legs, check, no head. You're definitely out of your body." The realization that she had died did not cause any concern at all; in fact, she was feeling "pretty great."

In the black void, she got a vague sense she was a body of light, and as she wondered what would happen next, something propelled her into an amazingly beautiful night sky. Lights that twinkled like stars surrounded her, connected by an intricate spider's web made up of colors she had never seen before. None of the constellations were familiar. They were completely different formations but seemed purposeful. "I felt separate at first," Deborah explained. "Then quickly I felt that not only was I part of this web of light, but I was an important part of that web."

Deborah was amazed to be a part of the web and felt so filled with wonder and awe, content to exist in this space without knowing how she got there or what it was. In fact, she didn't even want to try and figure it out. It didn't matter to her. Time was no longer a consideration, as it no longer existed. Everything was happening at the same moment. There was no past or future, just the eternal now. Her perception was different. No longer bound by a physical body, she was aware that her usual five senses did not apply to the space she was in, and could 'see' with panoramic, 360-degree vision.

She was aware of the lights and the web, "But I really wasn't seeing it with my eyes. In fact, at some point, the lights were so bright and beautiful that I remember saying to myself, don't look directly at them because they're so bright; they'll hurt your eyes," she recalled. "When that thought occurred, something pulled me to look directly at them, and I did. There was no sensation except amazement. It's almost like I could join with them, but it was more than that. I felt like there was no separation between my light and the others. We were one." Deborah felt the lights looked back at her with a boundless love, and could sense the deepest parts of her soul. It felt mutual, as though she had discovered a newfound ability to feel a love she had never been capable of experiencing before.

The entire expanse resonated with musical vibrations. Incredible harmonic and dissonant sounds worked together perfectly in an amazing, purposeful, and beautiful way. The harmonic sounds seemed to vibrate not only around her but also inside her, and she felt as though she was hearing them with her whole spirit. There was a great sense she had been here before and a strong, familiar feeling of 'coming home.'

Deborah rapidly accelerated across the web and realized that each gleaming light was a soul. She recognized some of them from her earthly life (or lives) but also felt that she knew all of them from another time and place and despite them all being unique, there was no separation. "I was connected to each one in a way that was just magnificent," she recalled.

The energy of one soul felt incredibly familiar, like a sister. Deborah found it confusing, as it didn't seem like her sister. She also sensed a clear connection between her mother and this soul, as if they were part of the same family. Her energy passed quickly.

"There were very rapid images of different events from the lives of those souls, from their physical and earthly lives." Amidst the scenes were births, deaths, struggles, and trauma. There were images from Deborah's life, but the focus was on the souls in the web. The experience moved too fast, and she wanted it to slow down, but she received a message that it was not the events that were important but the way the events affected the souls. As Deborah narrowed her view to focus on the beings of light, she received the message that the events could not harm the immortal souls. The soul was eternal and intact, and nothing could ever destroy it. Deborah felt comforted and relieved by this message.

"I was told repeatedly that none of these things can affect the soul," she explained. "This is who we are, who you are, and nothing that's happened to you in your own life can really affect this, except for the one thing that is most important to the soul. I thought, 'Well, what is that? What is that one thing?'" The speeding images slowed, and her life review began. As the scenes unfolded, some moments were painful to watch. Despite her anguish, she understood she was the one responsible for judging herself, not her guide or God. "I was shown some events where I could have made better choices. Some were painful, but I was shown these experiences through the experience of the other, so I felt what the other person was feeling as if it was me experiencing the effects of my actions" she explained. "I thought, 'Oh, please, you're not going to show me this. Do I have to see this?' But I did not feel I was being judged for any of it. I feared that I would be, but was told that I was being shown these things to learn important lessons."

One scene depicted her departure from a restaurant after having a meal with colleagues from Johns Hopkins. The restaurant provided a large amount of food, so they took some home in takeout containers. There was a homeless man sitting outside, and Deborah locked eyes with him. She knew he was hungry and considered giving him her food, but she thought of her children and took the food home. At that moment, in the life review, she was aware that this man felt not only hunger, but tremendous shame. The timeline of his life was clear to her. She witnessed his once-successful career and the tragic car accident that led to his addiction to pain medication, ultimately destroying his life and resulting in his homelessness. "So, the worst part of that for him was not that he was physically hungry and that I was not giving him the food. It was the tremendous shame and the judgment that he perceived I was making. It was incredibly painful for me to know."

As the experience continued, it became clear that this was not a courtroom but a classroom. The experience showed Deborah lives where people were being victimized, but also where their souls were the perpetrators. It was difficult for her to grasp the concept that the perpetrators were not judged, that there was a purpose for everything, and, ultimately, this was beneficial for all.

As her life review continued, she was shown events that highlighted actions of love and compassion. Some were simple events; some required great effort. She received the message that this is who we all are. This was our purpose, the essence of our creation. We embodied love and compassion; they defined who we were, and this is all that could really impact the soul. As the events played out, the lights became brighter, and their vibrations increased as their energy elevated. "I felt their happiness," she recalled. "This is where we came from, this is where we're going to return to, and this is really all that matters." A profound feeling of love consumed her, and the thought of leaving was unbearable.

Without warning, she moved away from the web and shifted close to two light beings. Their energy was familiar, and it appeared they had been waiting for her. One of them reached out to communicate, and Deborah realized he was the ICU patient who had seen her during his NDE in 1977. Her reaction to seeing him was a mix of surprise and excitement. "I was like, wow, it's really you," she recalled. "He was like, well, yes, of course it's me. I wouldn't be anywhere else. I am here to give you a message." He told her that her encounter with him when she was a junior nurse didn't happen by accident and that her mission was to share that experience. He said that sharing what had happened would help many people.

Deborah was excited to take on the mission but then realized she would have to return to her life and asked if someone else could do it as she wanted to stay. He said she had already agreed to return. She objected, stating definitively that she had made no decision to return. "He told me, 'It's okay.' You agreed to it. You have a choice, but you were given that choice and you've already agreed. You came from here; you're going to return here, and the truth is you're always here." She remained confused as his light faded and he moved away.

The second light moved forward, and Deborah recognized him as her deceased father. She was overwhelmed with love and gratitude to be in his presence and was even more determined to stay. He told her they could never truly be separated, that he didn't abandon her when he died, and when she returned to her life, they would still be together. He urged her not to be afraid to return to her body. Deborah didn't fully understand what he was saying but trusted him and felt that he would do nothing to harm her.

"I felt myself being pulled away from that place pretty quickly," she explained. "I found myself hovering above the ICU in the hospital. I could see my family outside the ICU in the waiting room with a basket of things they were all sharing while they waited, I was happy that they had some refreshments and things to snack on as I could see how upset they were."

She returned to her room. "I was hovering over the ICU bed, and I saw my body." They had hooked Deborah up to a ventilator, had many IV drips and medications running into her, and was on several critical care monitors. She had worked in this unit as a nursing supervisor and knew why those pieces of equipment were there. "I remember thinking, okay, I know what this means," she recalled. "I don't think they expect me to wake up, and this doesn't look good. So, guess what? I don't have to go back into that body again! I was very relieved."

The medical staff had taped her eyes closed and she knew that this indicated she had been in a coma. Doctors tape the eyes of comatose patients closed to prevent eye injury. Restraints were on her wrists, but she couldn't see if they were tied. As she looked down on herself, she felt her soul was too vast to be confined by her physical form but suddenly, she was in her body and had regained consciousness. She felt extremely confined, in great pain, and, for the first time during this experience, fear. Breathing was difficult, and she pulled out the endotracheal tube, setting off a flurry of alarms that brought nurses rushing to her bedside.

"I couldn't speak," she recalled. "I was thinking to myself, why are you looking at me like you saw a ghost? Why are you so shocked? I'm fine." Deborah still felt attached to the expansiveness of her spirit, and to the place she had just returned from. The nurses were asking orientation questions to test her awareness. She didn't answer them immediately, and the frustrated critical care physician asked her just to say anything, and she replied, "Well, I've had better days." The physician and nurse at her bedside appeared shocked. The doctor, with a look of surprise, turned to the nurse and said, "I can't believe it. I think she is going to be alright."

Deborah had suffered a brain injury and could not remember who the president was or what day of the week it was, but she could remember perfectly the entire near-death experience. Soon after waking, Deborah asked how she could go back to the spiritual place. As she described what had happened, the nurse said, "I think we need to give her some sedation."

She knew she had returned to her body, but she longed to go back to the universal place of light and love she had just left. Even though she was back, Deborah still felt a deep connection to the spirit world, and it took her a long time to integrate the transformative spiritual experience with her return to physical life. Since then, Deborah has believed that we are primarily spiritual beings, having a temporary physical experience on Earth to learn the lessons of unconditional love for the growth of our souls.

Verification Events

Johns Hopkins Patient

While Deborah was working as an intensive care nurse at Johns Hopkins, a patient went into cardiac arrest. The team tried to resuscitate the patient, but their efforts were unsuccessful. The chief resident said they were not making progress and should call the time of death. Deborah suggested they go one more round, and the chief resident agreed. The next attempt brought back his heartbeat. Two days later, when Deborah returned to the hospital, she visited the patient, and he accurately described the resuscitation. He recognized Deborah and thanked her for saying they should try one more round.

He described the lead resident with blood on his shirt. He correctly stated where Deborah was standing, her long hair falling forward and the team had problems inserting his endotracheal tube. He accurately described the anesthesiologist as a tall man wearing glasses, a blue hat, and blue scrubs. All of these observations were correct down to the finest detail

The descriptions accurately made by her patient, and later verified, were made while he was in full cardiac arrest. "Without a pulse or blood pressure there was no flow of blood or oxygen to his brain," Deborah explained. "Making it impossible for him to have a conscious experience during which he could make such observations, especially with such amazing accuracy. This suggests that consciousness is not produced by the brain, but filtered by it. Consciousness is universal and exists apart from our brains and physical bodies."

The Basket

While still out of her body, Deborah had seen her family sitting in the waiting room with a care basket and thought, "Well, where did they get that basket from?" She found out later that a friend had brought in a care basket with all kinds of things for her family. Two weeks after she regained consciousness, she asked her daughter, "Who brought that wonderful basket that you were using in the waiting room?" Her daughter asked, "Who told you about that?" Deborah replied, "Well, I saw you, and I could see what was in it." She went on to accurately describe its contents.

Deborah's Sister

During the experience, Deborah connected to a soul that had a sister's energy. This did not feel like the sister she had grown up with. Fifteen years later, Deborah received an email through the DNA testing service 23 and Me, "This may come as a shock, but we matched as a close-relatives. Please call me." Curious about her family history, Deborah reached out using the information provided, but nothing could have prepared her for what she would hear—nothing except for her near-death experience. Over the phone, a stranger explained that they were half-sisters, having matched as family. The caller revealed she had been adopted and had spent her life searching for her biological family. All the details of her adoption "clicked with her being the first biological child of my mother," Deborah explained. "At first, I was totally shocked, and then I remembered." In that moment, Deborah recalled the unfamiliar "sister energy" she had felt during her out-of-body experience. "I thought to myself, well, there you are, there you are."

Deborah discovered that her mother had given birth to her half-sister when she was 21 and unmarried, and had made the difficult decision to put her up for adoption. Neither Deborah nor her family knew anything about it, not even her extended family. Deborah had sensed "meeting her" in the spirit realm and felt her energy, but it wasn't until more than 15 years later, when DNA confirmed their biological connection, that she understood that "meeting."

*

Deborah had an out-of-body experience during a car accident when she was young, allowing her to observe events that were later confirmed by her father, who was with her when they were hit by a drunk driver. As a young ICU nurse, she was able to verify the details shared by a patient who had his own near-death experience while in full cardiac arrest. Many years later, during a full cardiac arrest of her own, she experienced a detailed and profound near-death experience when she had no pulse, blood pressure, or blood flow to her brain. She was clinically dead for about 20 minutes. The idea that these experiences were mere hallucinations doesn't hold up given the many details that were later validated as true by other people, medical staff, and the medical records.

4. Ancestral Guardian: The Mystery of Drake

VINCENT TOLMAN

'Can you tell me anything about Charles?' She replied, 'Oh, you mean great-grandpa Drake.' I was floored. That's when I realized I needed to get out of my own way, embrace the experience, and stop trying to explain it all."

*

On Saturday, January 18, 2003, Vincent Tolman woke up eager to make the most of his rare day off from his construction job. He had planned a full day with his close friend and gym partner, Rob. They had been going to the gym every day, pushing each other toward bigger goals and faster progress.

Vinny drove to Rob's place to pick him up. A new nutritional supplement they had ordered from Thailand had finally arrived. Both were excited to try it, believing it would help their muscles recover more quickly and allow them to keep up their workout schedule without rest days. What Vinny and Rob didn't realize was that supplements from Thailand were formulated differently than those manufactured in the United States. "Everything we were buying in the States was already diluted," Vinny explained. "In the United States, it was a 5% solution; the rest was water. The stuff outside the States we were buying was 100% solution. It was like taking 20 times the normal dose. That much in your system? It was toxic."

They each poured out what they guessed was a safe dose of the supplement and swallowed it down. Almost instantly, a strange sensation hit them, radiating from their stomachs and spreading through their bodies. The label on the bottle was entirely in Thai, leaving them unable to check if they'd taken the correct amount. Their only previous experience with side effects from supplements had been minor, and they'd found that eating something usually helped. Hoping this would work again, Vinny and Rob made their way to a nearby burger restaurant.

As they drove, however, the effects of the supplement took an unsettling turn. Rob, who was at the wheel, began nodding off, struggling to keep his eyes open. "So, I was shaking him awake," Vinny later recounted, "he was driving, and I was shaking him awake as we pulled into the parking lot." Vinny stepped out of the car, feeling dizzy, as he headed straight for the single-person bathroom inside the restaurant. He locked the door behind him, lost his balance, and collapsed backward, hitting the cold tile floor. In his dazed state, he vomited. Some of it, however, pooled in his throat, blocking his airway as he lay flat on his back and he lost consciousness.

Rob stumbled into the restaurant, reaching a booth before he, too, suffered from the effects of the supplement. He slumped over the table, vomited, and then collapsed in a heap. Alarmed, the restaurant staff quickly approached him, attempting to rouse him, but he did not respond. Realizing the severity of the situation, the manager immediately called 911, reporting a possible poisoning.

Since Vinny and Rob had arrived separately, no one in the restaurant realized Vinny was still in the locked bathroom. Later, Vinny recalled the strange sensations he experienced in that unconscious state. "The next thing I know, I'm starting to fall. I can feel myself falling. All of a sudden, everything went black. It felt like somebody dipped me in this cool pool of water."

It was a strange sensation, almost as if a current of small energy waves was carrying him. In the distance, a soft light appeared, growing gradually brighter. Suddenly, as if snapped into another realm, Vinny felt as though he was in a darkened movie theater, watching a scene unfold on the screen. But the scene was unsettling. He saw the image of a lifeless body sprawled on the floor of a restaurant bathroom, viewed from above. He watched, baffled by what he was seeing, unable to understand why he was witnessing this. It didn't even cross his mind that the body might be his own. He felt perfectly fine, watching from above, detached from the figure on the floor.

"The body didn't look normal," Vinny explained. "The neck had swollen up because the body had kind of struggled as it suffocated. The skin was almost turning yellow and purple, like literally there were blotches of yellow and blotches of purple. It didn't look real. It looked like a bad fake body from a movie or something. So, to me, it didn't even dawn on me at all that what I was looking at was my body. What I thought I was looking at was a movie."

Vinny drifted higher, looking down at the restaurant. He could see everything as if the roof had vanished, leaving each room visible below. He could see the kitchen, the booths, the bustling staff, and the bathroom where his own body lay still on the floor. Strangely, he could hear every thought of every person in the restaurant, a chaotic stream of inner voices layering over one another, yet each was distinct.

Despite the overwhelming sensation, he felt detached. He wondered why the "director" of this bizarre movie had chosen this overhead perspective and, even more puzzling, why everyone's thoughts were audible in the soundtrack. It felt too deliberate, like a scene designed to convey something profound, yet Vinny couldn't work out the message. He remained in his serene state, watching the unfolding events as though they were all part of a carefully crafted scene. A restaurant guest tried repeatedly to open the locked bathroom door. When he couldn't, he found the manager and explained that there might be someone inside who needed help, as he could hear a phone ringing with no one answering.

The manager hurried over with a key and unlocked the door. As it opened, he stopped, shocked to find Vinny's lifeless body sprawled on the floor, his neck visibly swollen. The manager quickly grabbed his phone and dialed 911 again. The operator began guiding the manager through emergency procedures to try to revive Vinny. One of the staff members reached down to check for a pulse but quickly recoiled, saying that Vinny's body felt stone cold. On hearing this, the operator instructed them to leave the bathroom and lock the door until the paramedics arrived. Within minutes, an ambulance pulled up outside, and three medics entered the restaurant. Two of them were seasoned veterans. The third, a young EMT in his first week.

Vinny explained the situation. "This is about 30 to 45 minutes after my buddy had already been taken away. So I've been down at least 45 minutes by the time the ambulance gets there. They made some preliminary attempts to try to resuscitate the body, but it was cold; it was dead. Even stiffness had formed in the joints. So they figured the body had been dead for at least a little bit, you know, maybe an hour or so." As Vinny watched, he felt an unexpected connection with the youngest medic, tuning in to his thoughts with surprising clarity. The young man felt waves of sadness and regret as he wondered if they could have done more to save him. Vinny sensed the medic's self-doubt as they placed him in the body bag, secured him to a board, and transferred him to the ambulance.

The police arrived soon after and completed the paperwork with the restaurant manager and ambulance crew. There was a lack of urgency, which weighed heavily on the young medic. The two experienced medics climbed into the front of the ambulance, the young EMT sat alone in the back, staring at the body bag. His thoughts flooded through to Vinny. "Did we give up too soon? Should I have pushed harder, tried something else?" It struck Vinny how deeply the young man cared, his mind cycling through scenarios and second-guessing each decision. As the ambulance moved just a few blocks away from the restaurant, Vinny noticed a strange phenomenon. The young medic's heart glowed, a soft, steady light emanating from his chest. From Vinny's otherworldly perspective, the light seemed to intensify. A powerful force swept up behind him and over his left shoulder as if something immense and purposeful was moving directly toward the medic. As the force touched the young medic, his heart's glow flared even brighter as though responding to the unseen energy.

Then, a booming voice rang out, "This one's not dead." Startled, the medic instinctively glanced around the ambulance, searching for the source of the voice, but eventually shrugged it off. Yet, the light from his heart continued to grow, now expanding beyond his chest to envelop his waist and stretch upward toward his head.

Just as Vinny wondered if this was an isolated event, he felt the force surge over his shoulder again, even stronger than before, and strike the young medic with more intensity. This time, the voice rang out with even greater power, "This one's not dead." As Vinny heard the words, he sensed that this was not a message. It was a command.

The young medic acted on an impulse. He loosened one strap, unzipped the body bag, and began feeling along Vinny's neck for any sign of a pulse. When he found none, he moved to check under the arm. Still, nothing. He unfastened another strap and pressed his fingers to an artery on the inside of Vinny's leg, pushing down hard. His fingers pressed so deeply that they contacted bone. In that instant, Vinny felt a powerful jolt. It was like a shock of electricity coursing through him.

"So, where I was up here watching this movie," Vinny later described, "I felt like a jolt, like somebody shocked me." For the first time since this strange journey began, Vinny felt something physical, and he noticed the medic seemed to experience it, too. The young man's eyes widened as if he, too, had felt that spark of life. Vinny was sharing in the medic's experience, feeling what he felt.

The young EMT pressed on. He placed an oxygen mask over Vinny's mouth and prepared the defibrillator. The moment the defibrillator's alarm went off, the two senior medics in the front looked at each other, immediately realizing what was happening in the back. They turned around and shouted at the young man, their voices filled with urgency. "What are you doing? Are you trying to get yourself fired?" one demanded. "You can't do this. It's illegal!" The other medic added, "They'll arrest you. We're not allowed to use a defibrillator on a declared body. You know that." But the young medic didn't stop.

Ignoring the voices from the front, the young man held his ground and delivered the first shock, but the monitor showed nothing. No sign of life. He quickly began charging the defibrillator for a second attempt. The older medic in the passenger seat, now fully alarmed, rose from his seat, intent on stopping him. Before he could reach him, the young EMT shocked Vinny again. For a fleeting moment, the monitor registered a single heartbeat before it flatlined. The senior medic froze. Maybe this was worth pursuing after all. The young medic delivered a third round, and this time, after the shock went through Vinny's chest, the monitor displayed a faint but steady heartbeat.

"Part of the miracle of all of this is that when the heart started, they were very close to a hospital," Vinny explained. "This hospital was so close they could pull right in, and they were able to radio ahead and have a team there ready to meet them so that they could begin to resuscitate this body or continue to help this body come back all the way. Oddly, even still at this point. I don't know that it's me. I really don't know that it's me."

As Vinny hovered, he sensed a deep joy radiating from the young medic as he realized he had succeeded in pulling someone back from the edge. But with Vinny regaining strength, his body suddenly convulsed, sending him into a series of seizures. The medical team quickly transferred him to a stretcher, strapping him down as his limbs thrashed uncontrollably. The moment the strap tightened over his left arm, Vinny felt something. He looked down and, to his astonishment, saw that this was his arm. This limb, with its familiar scars and muscles, was no longer distant. It was real and undeniably his. In that instant, everything clicked into place. The scenes he'd been observing weren't of a stranger. He had been watching his own death. This was his body, his life that had been slipping away and then pulled back.

"I started to see all the negative impacts I ever had in my life to anyone around me," he recalled. "It was so fast it was in an instant. But I saw everything. I saw every negative impact I ever had in my life. I saw every bad thing I ever did, every fight I've ever gotten into. Every time I cut someone off, flip someone on anything, anything I ever did bad, I saw it in my life. Then from there, I actually felt this feeling like you're not worth it. Like you've done all of this harm in this world. Why would you be worth saving?"

Gradually, he noticed a warmth behind him, softly at first, then steadily growing until it enveloped him. The warmth seemed to reach deep within him with a sense of calm he hadn't realized he needed. One by one, memories emerged, each filled with moments of kindness, laughter, and connection. He saw times when he'd helped friends, supported family members, and even small, seemingly insignificant gestures he had forgotten. He could see the ripple effect of these moments, how each thoughtful act had affected the lives of others, prompting more acts of kindness in return. For the first time, Vinny fully understood the impact he'd made. He saw how much light he'd spread through his actions, how those pleasant moments had shaped others' lives. He understood he was worth saving, that his life, imperfect as it was, had meaning and value.

The warmth intensified, flooding Vinny with an overwhelming sense of unconditional love. He turned to look behind him. What he saw left him breathless, or as close as a soul could be to being breathless. "I was amazed. It was so beautiful!" he later described. "If you could cry as a spirit, I was crying. You know, as a soul, I felt just that emotional stillness, that I was being loved like I'd never been loved in my whole life here." It was a love that completely filled him. At that moment, he felt whole, profoundly valued, and so peaceful that every past hurt, every sorrow, seemed to dissolve away.

As Vinny turned, he found himself face to face with an elderly gentleman. The man, impeccably dressed in a white suit and a flowing white robe radiated an aura of calmness and wisdom. Long, silvery-white hair cascaded down his shoulders, blending with a flowing beard. His skin was unlike anything Vinny had ever seen, a brilliant shade of pink. Every part of him seemed to emit a gentle, radiant glow.

Vinny understood that this man, this glowing presence, had been guiding the entire experience. It was the powerful voice Vinny had heard in the ambulance, "This one's not dead." The elderly man's eyes held a depth of compassion that surpassed anything Vinny had known, and he felt as if this being had known him forever. This luminous figure had carefully woven every detail, bringing him to this moment.

Vinny couldn't help but ask, "Are you God?" The man smiled and replied, "No." He asked, "Are you Jesus?" Again, the man responded, "No, I'm not Jesus. I'm here to be your helper, to be your guide." He then introduced himself, saying, "My name is Drake, and I'm here to be your escort, to help you go anywhere in the universe you want to go."

It was at that moment that Vinny realized something remarkable. Neither of them had been speaking out loud. "That's when I started to realize that he wasn't using his mouth at all, and I wasn't either," Vinny recalled later. "We were strictly communicating through thought. The second I had a thought, he heard it, and the second he had a thought, I heard it." Drake told Vinny he had a choice. He could return to his life, or he could remain in this place of peace and limitless love. However, if he returned, he was warned that it wouldn't be easy.

Life would come with challenges, perhaps harder than anything he had faced before, but he would have the strength to handle them. The desire to remain in that warmth, to surrender to the peace surrounding him, was almost overwhelming. Yet Vinny was acutely aware of his connection to his body. He could feel the sharp edges of physical pain, reminding him of the life he would have to endure if he returned. Through that connection, he sensed the medical team's efforts to revive him.

Drake offered to show Vinny what awaits beyond life, and without hesitation, Vinny agreed. But rather than traveling from one physical place to another, Vinny realized they were moving from one level of understanding to a higher one. As they ascended through these layers, Drake explained, "As we raise your understanding or raise your knowledge, we're going to raise your ability to embrace truth." Each step upward seemed to lift Vinny's entire being, expanding his capacity for insight. "We're going to raise your frequency," Drake continued, "and that's going to help us get to where we want to go."

Vinny saw that what he understood as "heaven" was not a place to be reached by physical travel but a state of profound awareness and higher frequency. "I got to go to heaven," he later reflected, "but you know, heaven is not something you just take a spaceship to. You have to reach this much higher place, this elevated way of living or being, to even be able to experience it."

Each new level revealed dimensions of truth and love more powerful than the last. It was as though his entire spirit was being tuned to resonate at a higher frequency. In this space, Drake told Vinny that he would need to comprehend several eternal truths. With each new truth, Vinny's understanding expanded, but the concepts felt almost out of reach. The shift to a higher frequency wasn't easy. Drake saw Vinny was challenged and simplified the lesson, breaking the truths down in a way that helped Vinny to grasp each one fully.

As Vinny opened himself to these insights, he found they propelled him to a higher vibration. This place of heightened frequency appeared similar to Earth, yet it had an intensity unlike anything Vinny had ever seen. Colors were more vibrant, sounds resonated at deeper levels, and even the air felt charged with energy. In this heightened realm, Vinny saw Earth for what it truly was: a dim reflection of this higher plane, existing on a lower, denser frequency.

The truths Drake shared took on a new meaning, as if they were more than teachings. Here, everything existed at a heightened level of purpose and harmony, a dimension that Vinny now saw as the true nature of existence. "Drake helped me get an understanding of the cosmos and Earth's place in the cosmos," Vinny explained. "We're one bead of sand on the beach, and all the other grains of sand are other life forms. There's so many forms of life in the universe. There's energetic bodies, there's light bodies, there's Wisp bodies, there's so many different forms of life. There's more forms of life than we could even imagine with our imagination, literally more than we could imagine."

Drake guided Vinny to a breathtaking landscape. As he took in his surroundings, he felt a powerful wave of love radiating from everything around him. The grass, the flowers, the trees, and the gentle flow of the water all seemed to embrace him in an overwhelming sense of love.

At the summit of a nearby hill, Vinny saw a magnificent building of gleaming white marble. People moved in and out through doorways that materialized only as they aligned with each person's unique frequency, guiding them directly to the rooms they needed. As they stepped inside, each entrance vanished behind them. Vinny felt it was a space of complete enlightenment where one could pursue knowledge with no outside influence. As he watched, he recognized individuals from across history, as if every era he had ever read about had converged here.

He saw ancient Romans, figures from the 1600s through to the 1800s, and even people dressed in contemporary clothing, representing a vast spectrum of cultures, beliefs, and traditions. "I was really amazed at how inclusive this space was, that anybody who wanted to go there who matched the love frequency could go there. And it was just a beautiful thing that heaven is for all of us," Vinny recalled. "That wasn't necessarily the destination heaven or the heaven where people go to kind of stay awhile. That was the heaven for learning."

Drake led Vinny to areas where spirits lived in the eras they most deeply identified with. These places radiated peace, entirely free from the harm and dark energy of the Earth. Here, people found rest, healing, and joy. In these settings, they prepared for the next stage of their journey. Drake embraced him, and Vinny felt their energy merge, becoming a single, unified presence. Drake looked at him and said, "This is going to be very hard, but it's going to be worth it."

Suddenly, Vinny heard his brother's voice, softly praying beside his hospital bed. As his brother whispered, "Amen," Vinny felt himself pulled back into his body. After three days in a coma he awoke. An intense sense of claustrophobia overwhelmed him. Without hesitation, he removed the IVs and swung his legs over the edge of the bed, moving swiftly toward the door. As he reached the elevator, an alarm sounded, drawing the attention of a nurse, who quickly found Vinny attempting to leave. "She walked into the room and immediately thought someone must have stolen the body, assuming I'd be in a coma for the rest of my life. But there I was, standing right in front of her," Vinny recalled with a smile.

The hospital staff, surprised, insisted he undergo a series of tests before considering discharge. Vinny's neurologist was baffled and said that there was no scientific explanation for Vinny's recovery. Word of his awakening spread quickly, and soon, the entire floor was talking about him as "the miracle boy." Despite their concerns, Vinny remained adamant about going home. Reluctantly, they agreed and discharged him on his own recognizance.

Verification Events

Drake

Vinny traveled to Star Valley, Wyoming, for a family reunion, where he attended a presentation at a local school. A video screen displayed historical images of prominent town figures. Suddenly, an image appeared that made Vinny catch his breath. It was unmistakably Drake, his spiritual guide. Underneath the photo, however, was the name "Charles Cazier." Though puzzled by the name, he knew it was Drake. Vinny remembered that his grandmother's maiden name was Cazier and decided to ask her about the man in the picture. "The next day, I had the chance to talk to her," Vinny recounted. "I asked, 'Can you tell me anything about Charles?' She replied, 'Oh, you mean great-grandpa Drake.' I was floored. That's when I realized I needed to get out of my own way, embrace the experience, and stop trying to explain it all." Drake was his great-great-great-grandfather. Vinny realized Drake had been watching over him throughout his life.

Psychiatrist

Shortly afterward, Vinny met with a psychiatrist who dismissed his experience as a delusion. The psychiatrist insisted that if near-death experiences (NDEs) were real, science would have validated them with research by now. But near the end of their session, Vinny suddenly sensed the presence of the psychiatrist's grandmother in the room. She shared with him a few intimate, loving details from the psychiatrist's past, memories so personal that not even his wife, children, or other family members knew of them. When Vinny relayed this information, the psychiatrist's initial reaction was shock and anger, and he quickly asked Vinny to leave. Yet, minutes later, the psychiatrist called him to apologize, admitting he had forgotten about those memories, as they were buried in his youth. Before they ended the call, the psychiatrist advised Vinny to continue on this journey without medication, acknowledging that this path was one Vinny needed to explore on his own.

Medic

Vinny met the young medic for lunch, hoping to confirm details about what had happened in the ambulance. But each time Vinny brought it up, the medic would grow visibly emotional, struggling to find his words. When Vinny mentioned watching him opening the body bag, the medic's reaction was immediate. He grew overwhelmed, clearly finding it difficult to revisit that moment. Whatever had occurred left a deep impact on both of them.

Reference

Vincent Tolman, Lynn Taylor, (2022) *'The Light After Death: My Journey To Heaven and Back',* Ascendt Publishing

5. The Socks That Confirmed Eternity

TIBOR PUTNOKI

Tibor accurately described the actions of a nurse in a room next to the ward, separated by a two-way mirror. This made it impossible for him to see into the room, yet he witnessed specific details.

*

Tibor Putnoki was born in 1946 in Mándok, Hungary. Growing up in an orphanage, he quickly learned to rely on himself, developing a strong sense of independence from a young age. At 16, Tibor discovered a passion for aviation when he learned to fly small aircraft. As he got older, he faced serious health challenges, including multiple sclerosis, and later, a back injury left him with partial paralysis.

In 1994, Tibor was admitted to a Hungarian hospital's intensive care unit due to dangerously high blood pressure. His bed was the middle one of three in the small ICU ward. After several tests, a doctor told him his condition was critical and his chances of survival were slim. Soon after the doctor's warning, Tibor felt a sharp tearing pain in his chest. As the pain intensified, he feared for his life. But in an instant, the pain vanished, replaced by an overwhelming sense of wellbeing. "I felt better than I have ever felt," Tibor recalled, "as if everything had been relieved." In that moment, he heard nothing, but the silence felt deeply meaningful. The stillness was suddenly broken by the loud alarms of two monitors. Medical staff rushed in and immediately began CPR.

As Tibor watched from a detached perspective, he felt curious about the commotion. He could see the doctor performing chest compressions on the patient lying in the bed. "This patient is lucky to have such a good doctor," he thought to himself. "But it was strange because this young kind man is furious," Tibor recalled. "He's shouting; he was yelling at the nurse, 'Do it fast.' He was giving the injection to the man. Maybe it was because he was yelling at her, but the nurse didn't give the injection, and the vein collapsed. I'm sure that this patient is a VIP patient. But the doctor is shouting that out. 'Please bring another nurse from the preparatory room!' It was by the side of our room. It was a mirror wall. From there, they could see in, but we could not see them from our bed." As the doctor continued to shout and call for help, Tibor wondered what the preparatory room looked like, he had the odd sensation of the air around him vibrating and, in an instant, found himself there.

He was standing behind a nurse, who was rapidly pulling supplies from a cabinet and placing them on a trolley. She didn't seem to notice him at all, as if he were invisible. A small brown package slipped from her hand and bounced under the glass cabinet. Without attempting to retrieve it, she simply grabbed another package from the cabinet and placed it on the trolley. Curious, Tibor moved closer to examine the package the nurse had dropped. He saw it contained a large injection needle. There was lettering printed on one side of the package and a serial number on the other. At that moment, Tibor realized he had been watching everything from an unusual perspective, with the surrounding walls not blocking his view. A buzzer sounded, and a display indicated a patient in the third ward room needed help.

Intrigued by the alert, Tibor felt the surrounding air vibrate and instantly, he stood beside an iron bed where a patient was anxiously pressing the emergency button. He watched the man with a calm curiosity as he realized he could be wherever he focused his attention. "I'm standing by the side of the iron bed. There was a patient, and he was pushing the button. Looking at him, I was questioning. Why'd you push the bell? Because there is no problem." Just then, a nurse hurried into the room, coming to stand right beside Tibor as if he were invisible. She asked the patient what was wrong, and he replied that he was thirsty. The nurse quickly poured him a glass of water, handed it to him, and left without acknowledging Tibor. Watching this, Tibor realized she hadn't noticed he was there.

The air vibrated, and Tibor found himself back in the preparatory room. He saw that the nurse had finished arranging everything on the trolley and was now on the phone. She sounded frustrated, and somehow, Tibor instinctively knew she was speaking to her husband. "She's talking with a flustering voice. I knew that this was her husband. The nurse says, 'I know the kids are sick. They have a fever. On the table, there's a phone book and the pediatrician's name; just call him!' In the next moment, I can feel this vibration and I'm in the city of Solanke."

Inside the nurse's apartment, Tibor watched the husband grow more and more frustrated as he searched through the phone book for the pediatrician's number. Tibor, seeing the man's struggle, tried to help and said, "It's on the first page." In a burst of anger, the husband threw the phone book to the floor. It landed open, with the pediatrician's number visible. Tibor took this moment to look around the apartment. He noticed the cherry nut wardrobes and the soft texture of the carpet and saw the books neatly arranged on the shelves. His eyes then landed on the husband's socks, which were decorated with small animal pictures. Tibor, slightly amused, thought to himself, "What kind of man wears socks like that? Something's not quite right with him."

In an instant, Tibor was back in the hospital ward, where he saw the medical staff still working on the "VIP" patient. He approached the bed to see who this important figure was. As he looked down, he was stunned to see his own face staring back at him. At that moment, a voice echoed clearly, saying, "Your time is up. You're going to die." Despite the weight of these words, Tibor felt a profound sense of peace. He was "free and easy," without pain or worry, experiencing a calm unlike anything he'd known. The nurse from the preparatory room entered quickly, pushing the trolley of supplies. Tibor began speaking to her, insisting, "Do nothing, leave me alone. I'm fine." But to his shock, the nurse walked right through him. A wave of horror washed over him. "It was really terrible," he later described. "I was horrified. It was a nightmare!"

Tibor turned to the doctor, desperately trying to communicate, but the doctor couldn't hear him. When he reached out to touch him, his hand passed right through. Fear gripped Tibor as he worried he had indeed died and was now trapped on Earth, unable to connect with anyone around him. His mind drifted to moments from his life, memories of actions and decisions he wasn't proud of.

As Tibor's fear grew stronger, a light appeared above him, and with it came an overwhelming sense of love and peace. The light drew closer, and he sensed a spiritual being. They rose effortlessly, passing through the ceiling. Looking down, he saw his own body lying on the bed below. It was then that he realized he was no longer connected to it. "It's like you take your clothes off and don't care about them," he later explained.

As he rose higher, he gazed down at the entire surgical unit. He could see each patient in their bed. He somehow knew everything about them, including the date of their death. This knowledge came to him without effort, an understanding that felt as natural as the light surrounding him. As Tibor rose high enough to view the entire city, he laughed. From his elevated viewpoint, he could see into people's homes, watching how they lived, aware of the intimate details of the countless lives below. But in an instant, his location shifted, and he felt himself moving through a vast space filled with a serene blue light.

His movement stopped, and he found himself in what he described as a 'big hole.' "Along one wall, I could see a projector with a screen and a movie's on, and a strange feeling came. It's not a movie, it's my life! From when I was born until I was passing away. There was a white screen, and above it, there was a narrow screen." The lower screen showed what had actually happened at each moment of his life. The upper screen depicted what he 'should' have done in those same moments. As Tibor watched the scenes from his life unfold, he saw each mistake and every good deed. He revisited his childhood in an orphanage, recalling the loneliness and the belief he had that he had no one to care for him. Over time, this belief led him to feel that he didn't need anyone, shaping much of his life's choices.

As Tibor watched his life review, he noticed a presence standing behind him. This presence radiated unconditional support and did not judge him for his past actions. At that moment, Tibor realized this presence had always been with him. It had guided and supported him throughout his life, and he hadn't noticed. Tibor felt ashamed that he had been oblivious to this spiritual guide. When the life review ended, he felt an overwhelming sense of failure and feared that punishment awaited him for his mistakes. But to his surprise, the life review began again. This time, Tibor saw his interactions with everyone he had ever met, not just from his own perspective but through the lens of their emotions. He felt the hurt, sadness, and disappointment he had caused whenever he was mean or rude. The emotional pain he felt was profound as he realized how his actions had impacted others more deeply than he had understood in life.

The spirit guide asked him three questions.

The first question was, "Did you have a life before your death?" Reflecting on his experiences and choices, Tibor answered, "No."

The second question followed, "Did you live a life worthy of a human being?" Once again, Tibor answered. "No."

Finally, the presence asked, "Could you look into your fellow beings' eyes with a pure heart and your head held high?" Tibor answered, "No."

These questions cut to the heart of his life's purpose and meaning. With each "no," Tibor felt the pain of having lived without fully embracing compassion and connection with others. His answers revealed to him the gap between the life he thought he had lived and the life he had actually led. As Tibor's second life review ended, he braced himself for the punishment he felt he deserved. But he heard a voice, immense, yet deeply calming, assuring him, "There is no problem. Everything can be redeemed."

The guide moved Tibor upward and together they travelled to a radiant city of light, where many people had gathered to greet him. The people welcomed him with love, telling him they had been waiting for him and he felt as if he were home. At that moment, he understood he belonged there. As Tibor's movement stopped, he noticed a barrier between himself and the city of light. He wanted to pass through, but the barrier was impenetrable. His guide explained, "You cannot enter this place." Confused, Tibor argued that he had made no decision that would prevent him from entering. But the presence calmly repeated, "The decision has been made."

Everything faded away, and a deep sense of unhappiness washed over Tibor as he found himself back in the hospital. The spirit guide was still beside him and together, they watched the doctor attempting to revive him. When the doctor eventually stopped, Tibor could feel the doctor's frustration and self-directed anger at being unable to resuscitate his patient. Tibor turned to the guide and asked for a purpose, a job he could fulfill on Earth. The presence simply told him, "Be happy." A sensation of a heavy weight pressed on Tibor's chest, and he joined his body again. He could hear the doctor's voice calling out, "He's alive! He's alive!"

The heart monitor had recorded a full nine minutes with no heartbeat. After Tibor had rested for a few hours, the doctor returned to his bedside with a pencil and notebook in hand. To Tibor's surprise, the doctor sat down and asked him directly, "What happened during those nine minutes?" The doctor noted down every detail as Tibor recounted his experience, from his out-of-body observations to his journey to the city of light and the spirit that had guided him.

In the preparatory room, the doctor reached under the cabinet and retrieved the package Tibor had described. Upon inspecting it, he found the writing and numbers to be exactly as Tibor had said. The doctor remarked that Tibor could not have known these details, as he had been performing CPR on Tibor when the package had fallen. Wanting to verify more of Tibor's descriptions, the doctor asked the assisting nurse if she knew him, to which she replied, "No." Then he read Tibor's description of her apartment aloud, and she confirmed it was accurate. When questioned about the phone conversation with her husband, she acknowledged that it had taken place exactly as Tibor described. The nurse took the doctor to her apartment to verify the details Tibor had given. When they returned to the hospital, the doctor held in his hand the pair of socks adorned with animal pictures, just as Tibor had described.

Verification Events

In Tibor's experience, he showed a remarkable ability to observe objects and events in detail, which he later described with striking accuracy. What makes this especially noteworthy is that several of these objects and events were not within his physical proximity or line of sight, even if he had been conscious.

The Preparatory Room

Tibor accurately described the actions of a nurse in a room next to the ward, separated by a two-way mirror. This made it impossible for him to see into the room, yet he witnessed specific details, such as the nurse dropping a medical package. Later, when the doctor retrieved the package from under the cabinet, he confirmed that the numbers and writing on it matched exactly as Tibor had reported.

The Nurse

Another striking element of Tibor's experience was his awareness of the nurse's phone conversation with her husband. Tibor not only described the content of the call, detailing that she was instructing her husband to look up a pediatrician's number for their sick children but also accurately conveyed her emotional state, noting her frustration and concern. When the doctor later asked the nurse about the call, she confirmed the conversation had occurred exactly as Tibor described.

Tibor accurately described the nurse's apartment, located miles from the hospital. At the very moment the doctor was performing CPR on Tibor in the hospital, Tibor described himself as being in the apartment, observing the nurse's husband while he searched for the pediatrician's number during the phone call. He provided precise details: the style of their wardrobes, the books on their shelves, the color and texture of the carpet, and the husband's unusual socks adorned with animal pictures. When the doctor inquired about Tibor's familiarity with the nurse or her home, she confirmed she did not know him and that he had never visited her apartment.

Conclusion

Tibor Putnoki's case presents a significant challenge to conventional neuroscience and the understanding of consciousness. His ability to perceive specific details, such as the actions and conversations in the preparatory room, the nurse's phone call to her husband, and even the detailed layout of an apartment miles away, occurred while he was in cardiac arrest, a state where brain activity is severely compromised, if not entirely absent. Tibor's experience includes many verifiable details, which the doctor and nurse later confirmed. These insights, occurring without the support of a functioning brain, strongly imply that his consciousness was operating independently of his physical body.

6. Lost in the City of Eternity

RANDY SCHIEFER

Randy felt a sense of verification. "She just verified everything that I experienced," he said.

*

In March 2020, Randy Schiefer began experiencing troubling symptoms. He felt unusually tired and nauseous, and he noticed that his sense of smell had disappeared entirely. Concerned, Randy visited his doctor and asked to be tested for COVID-19. However, the doctor refused, insisting that the virus wasn't present in their area. Instead, the doctor suggested it was likely just the flu and told Randy to go home and rest.

Two days later, Randy's condition worsened. He developed severe diarrhea, his nausea intensified to where he couldn't eat, and he felt completely drained of energy. Desperate for answers, Randy returned to the doctor. Once more, the doctor said he didn't have COVID-19 and refused to test him.

Shortly after, Randy's eldest daughter, Erin, came to visit him. Alarmed by how sick he looked, his labored breathing, and the grayish color of his skin, she immediately called her sister, Lisa, who was a nurse. "Dad is really sick," Erin said urgently. "He can hardly breathe, and he looks gray."

Lisa urged Erin to get their father to the hospital as soon as possible. Doctors admitted him on March 26th, quickly diagnosed him with bilateral pneumonia, and put him on oxygen. He was placed in isolation after X-rays showed his lungs were clouded with the characteristic "ground-glass" opacities linked to COVID-19. Within forty-eight hours, Randy's COVID-19 test returned positive.

Later that day, a doctor informed Randy that his oxygen levels were dangerously low. "My blood oxygen levels were down into the low 70s and they needed to put me on a ventilator," Randy recalled. "As a part of that, they had to put me to sleep. So they medically induced coma and intubated me." Within thirty-six hours, the ventilator was running at full capacity to sustain his oxygen levels. A doctor called Randy's family with a grim update. Randy's chances of survival were estimated at just 3%. The doctor recommended transferring Randy to a larger hospital with an ECMO machine (Extracorporeal Membrane Oxygenation). This heart-lung bypass system could provide the critical support his body needed.

Upon arrival at the new facility, Randy's condition took a severe turn. He suffered complete respiratory failure, and his health continued to rapidly decline. His kidneys soon failed, requiring dialysis to keep him stable. As his body struggled, his heart became enlarged and weakened, unable to pump blood effectively, and to make matters worse, his liver began producing blood clots.

At some point during his coma, Randy had four episodes of NDE. "I remember waking up; my consciousness came back," Randy recalls. "I was fully aware that I had died. I remember thinking to myself, you're dead. You know you've died." He moved slowly through an unusual tunnel. It looked like the interior of a passenger aircraft with all the seats removed, stretching endlessly into the distance. Multicolored light streamed through the small windows evenly spaced along either side. "The tunnel itself was rather dark. But you could feel the warmth, and the peacefulness and the love of this light that encased the tunnel that I was moving through."

Suddenly, he stood on a mezzanine floor in a magnificent golden hall. The walls gleamed in varying shades of gold, on each side, three grand archways led into different parts of the building, each outlined with intricate patterns of luminous golden stones. Massive, ornate chandeliers hung from the ceiling. Elegant water features dotted the hall while vast stained-glass windows lining the walls bathed the room in radiant, loving light, creating a warm and inviting presence.

Randy sensed someone beside him. "I didn't know who they were, but their presence brought me peace and comfort," he recalls. The man had dark hair, a dark beard, and wore a robe of rich colors. He looked at Randy with kindness and explained that this was one of his favorite rooms, the

"Welcoming Room." For several minutes, they talked about the hall's beauty. Then, the man looked at Randy with a serious expression and said unexpectedly, "You don't belong here yet. You need to leave." Randy continued, "He pointed to some big, beautiful oak doors. I remember my consciousness moving out through those doors and down some steps into a beautiful city."

Randy felt an overwhelming sense of homecoming as he wandered through the streets. The skyscrapers rose high above him, their tops disappearing into the sky. The city was warm and welcoming, filled with lush, green parks. Despite how familiar everything seemed, something didn't feel quite right. As he walked deeper into the city, Randy felt lost. Although he was in a place that should have felt like home, he couldn't shake the feeling of disorientation. The vastness of the city left him unsure of where to go next.

Panic set in as he realized he did not know how to find his way back. He sat down on a curb, and tears filled his eyes. He sensed others around him. Though aware of their energy, he couldn't make out their forms. The area was bustling with activity, yet no one offered help. "I remember sitting there on the curb, panicking," he recalls. "I was calling out to these people I couldn't see, yelling, 'Help me, I'm lost. Can someone please help me? Please!' But no one responded."

Desperate for a way out, Randy looked over his shoulder and found a beautiful staircase rising into the sky. He began to climb. "It felt like I was almost crawling up the staircase.

But it wasn't physical. I didn't feel like I had a body. It was just my consciousness, slowly moving up each step." He couldn't gauge how far he had climbed or how long he'd been there when, suddenly, he heard the familiar voice of the man he had met earlier, calling out, "There's Randy, get him!" Without warning, someone grabbed him by the collar and yanked him backward, pulling him off the staircase. As this happened, darkness and silence surrounded him, and he returned to the hospital to his unconscious body.

Some time later, Randy regained awareness and once more found himself in the mysterious city. He remembered the location of the staircase and made his way back to it, determined to climb. As he began his ascent, he again heard a voice calling out, "There's Randy, get him!" He looked back and saw a figure with white hair, a white beard, and dressed in a white robe with a beautifully crafted white sash around his waist. The man reached out and pulled Randy off the staircase. As soon as he felt the touch, Randy was abruptly pulled back into darkness, slipping once more into his unconscious, sedated state.

The next time Randy surfaced from his sleep, he was walking along a dirt path lined with vibrant flowers and tall trees. A certainty settled over him. "I must have died," he thought. A small boy appeared in front of him. "He had what we call a bowl haircut," Randy recalled. "Dark hair, olive skin, no shirt on, just a little pair of shorts. He was barefoot and full of energy." The boy was excited, eagerly gesturing to Randy, calling out, "Follow me! Follow me!"

The boy led Randy into a stunning room filled with red pedestal chairs arranged in neat rows, each one facing a large picture window that overlooked a breathtaking view. Just outside, a river flowed beneath the building, winding its way into the distance. Along its banks were many flowers. Randy watched people in the river, laughing and enjoying the water, while others sat along the riverbank, chatting and relaxing. The boy departed with a promise to return soon, leaving Randy alone. He felt perfectly content, captivated by the scene through the window. Time slipped by. Whether he waited five minutes or five hours, Randy couldn't tell.

Eventually, the boy reappeared, his expression regretful. "I'm sorry," he said. "You have to leave." Randy looked at the boy and pleaded to stay, expressing how calm, welcomed, and deeply loved he felt in this place. "This area is so beautiful," he told the boy. "I don't want to leave." The boy looked at him with understanding but remained firm. "No, I'm sorry," he replied. "Your room isn't ready. You have to leave." Randy fell back into his dreamless sleep.

Again, he surfaced into awareness. He found himself back in the strange tunnel, but this time, he was at its end. He stepped forward into a dark, shadowy void reminiscent of late dusk when shapes and figures blur and only faint outlines were visible. In the dimness, he sensed a presence beside him. Without speaking, the figure communicated telepathically and asked Randy to follow. Guided by this silent invitation, he moved forward through the shadows.

As they ventured deeper into the void, Randy noticed orbs of light whizzing past, filling the space with an ethereal energy. He explained, "One of the things I found in heaven is this incredible, 360-degree awareness. You can feel everything happening around you, you see it, you sense it. It's completely different from our experience here on Earth. Here, we're so confined by our limited vision, our restricted senses, and our physical energy. But in heaven, all of that is released, and you feel completely free. It's an entirely different sensation, unlike anything we know on Earth."

A small light appeared in the distance, gradually growing brighter until it illuminated a figure. "Suddenly, there stood my deceased mother-in-law," Randy recalled. "She looked beautiful, much younger than when she passed at 70. Here, she looked like she was in her 30s." She sat elegantly on a chair. A white ribbon held her hair neatly styled in a bun. She wore a stunning white robe with a delicate sash around her waist. Randy called out to his mother-in-law, hoping for a response. She glanced in his direction but then looked away. His guide subtly signaled that it was time to continue moving deeper into the void.

As they pressed forward, Randy suddenly noticed his deceased brother-in-law dash past. Though he had died in his mid-30s, he appeared here as a teenager. "I yelled out to him," Randy remembered, "but he didn't stop. He just ran right by without acknowledging me and kept going. But I could see him, saw his face, though not as clearly as my mother-in-law's.

Her face was so perfectly defined, so vivid, it felt like she was only two feet away from me."

Randy's guide urged him to continue. As they proceeded, the light around his mother-in-law slowly faded, eventually disappearing into complete darkness. In the distance, however, another faint light emerged, growing brighter as they approached. Soon, Randy recognized familiar faces: his mother, father, and sister, all of whom had passed years before.

Filled with excitement, he began calling out to them. "I was so thrilled to see them," he said. "I was just screaming and yelling, 'It's me! It's Randy! I'm here!'" But as he called to them, Randy felt a barrier separating him from his family. A sudden worry crept in. Was this barrier blocking his voice? They didn't look over or acknowledge his presence, and he feared they couldn't hear him.

Later, Randy's daughters shared a perspective that offered some comfort and understanding. They suggested that his family hadn't acknowledged him because they didn't want him to cross over the veil of death. They sensed he wasn't meant to be there yet. Perhaps, they suggested, his sudden presence had taken everyone by surprise, and in their silence, they were guiding him back to the life he still had to live.

An orb of light appeared in the distance, swiftly moving toward Randy. As it approached, a male face briefly materialized within the light, though Randy didn't recognize him. A message came through, "Tell Madison at the salon her grandfather's okay." Along with the message, the word 'veteran' resonated powerfully within him. "The word 'veteran' just permeated me," Randy recalled, "repeating over and over, filling me with its presence." The orb then drifted toward a white porch, where Randy saw the man making red, white, and blue ribbons alongside American flags.

At that moment, Randy's spirit guide told him it was time to leave. Before he could react, everything shifted, and he was abruptly drawn back into his coma.

*

Randy's daughter, Lisa, took charge of advocating for him to receive convalescent plasma treatment, which contained COVID-19 antibodies, a procedure still in its experimental phase. To proceed, Lisa had to get emergency authorization for use from the Federal Drug Administration, but Lisa and Randy's wife were determined. They found a local donor who had recovered from COVID-19 and was a perfect blood type match for Randy. After securing approval, Randy received the convalescent plasma on Good Friday, April 10th, becoming the first patient in Northwest Florida to undergo the treatment. Remarkably, within two days, on Easter Sunday, his lungs had cleared enough that doctors began weaning him off the ECMO machine. One week after receiving the plasma, Randy was completely off life support.

When Randy emerged from the coma, the hospital allowed his daughter, Lisa, to visit him. Eager to share what he had experienced, Randy told her, "I traveled. I went somewhere." But

Lisa, trying to make sense of his words, responded, "Dad, you were in a coma; you didn't go anywhere."

Randy soon realized that the hospital staff were also unprepared to understand or acknowledge his experience. "I wanted to talk to somebody about this because I didn't know what had happened," he recalled. "I mentioned it to a couple of nurses, and they just smiled and shook their heads. Then a doctor came in, and I started to tell him about the golden room I had seen. He just replied, 'Boy, you had quite a journey,' and walked out without really acknowledging what I was trying to share."

During his hospital stay, Randy received powerful drugs like ketamine, which triggered some vivid hallucinations. "I can tell the difference, you know, between my NDE and my hallucinations," Randy explained. "When I look up at the ceiling and see six dancing panda bears, well, yeah, that's a hallucination. I had a few other funny ones, too, like one of my doctors, who I thought was across the hallway playing with my dogs."

But Randy knew that his near-death experiences felt entirely different from these drug-induced visions. "I tried so hard to explain to someone who wasn't familiar with near-death experiences exactly how it felt and what I experienced," he shared. Randy admits he has only a vague sense of how his experiences unfolded during his coma. "I have no idea at what point in time any of this happened when I was in that coma. I don't know the sequence of events," he reflects. "Whether my visit to the hall came last or the message from Madison's grandfather came first, I have no clue."

Randy was in hospital for 44 days, from the 26th of March until the 9th of May, during which he was in a coma for 22 days. "I had to learn to walk again, and I had to learn to swallow. I have had to learn to talk because my voice was damaged from being intubated for so long."

Verification Events

Madison

Shortly after returning home, Randy was in his bedroom and felt an urge to rummage through a drawer filled with odds and ends. "Something drew my attention. I was here in my bedroom, in my wheelchair, and something drew me to that dresser." He wasn't searching for anything in particular, but as he sifted through the contents, he stumbled on a business card for a local salon. Realizing he needed a haircut, he asked his wife to call and check if they were open, given the COVID-19 lockdown restrictions. A few minutes later, his daughter Lisa came into his room, holding the card, her expression serious. She started asking him questions. "Where did you get this card? How long have you had it? Where did you find it?"

Confused, Randy replied, "Lisa, where is this going? I don't know where I got the card. I found it in the drawer. I don't think I've ever seen it before." After a moment of silence, Lisa looked at him thoughtfully. "Dad," she said, "I think we found your Madison."

Lisa handed the card to her father, and Randy noticed the name 'Madison' written on it, a hairdresser at the salon. Feeling the weight of the message he had received from her grandfather during his near-death experience, Randy asked Lisa to book him an appointment with Madison. He felt a strong responsibility to deliver the message, hoping it might provide comfort or meaning.

After waiting briefly at the barbershop, a young woman approached Randy, introducing herself. "Hi, I'm Madison. I think you're my next appointment." Lisa took a moment to explain Randy's recent illness and his time in the hospital.

Randy asked Madison if he could ask her some personal questions, and she said yes. He began, "Madison, are both of your grandfathers still alive?" Madison replied, "No, the grandfather I was closest to passed away less than a year ago." Randy continued, "Was your grandfather a veteran?" Madison nodded, explaining that her grandfather had served in the army and was a Vietnam veteran.

Randy had considered the possibility that he might have unconsciously recognized Madison's grandfather from somewhere around town. Hoping to clarify, he asked, "Did your grandfather ever live around here?" Madison shook her head, explaining that he had lived 1,100 miles away in Iowa and had never visited the area. Randy said, "I think your grandfather came to me with a message for you." He recounted his experience, explaining, "He approached me and said, 'Tell Madison at the salon her grandfather is okay.' I want you to know that, that he is okay."

As the message sank in, Madison's eyes filled with tears, and soon they were both crying. Lisa, overcome with emotion, joined in. Randy shared another detail with Madison, explaining, "I saw your grandfather on a white porch." Madison replied, "He had a white porch at his house in Iowa. After he retired, he loved sitting out there, talking to people as they walked along the sidewalk."

Randy described how he had seen her grandfather making red, white, and blue ribbons and American flags. Madison explained, "He belonged to the local American Legion. Every Veterans Day, our whole family would go there to make red, white, and blue ribbons and flags for the veterans." Randy felt a sense of verification. "She just verified everything that I experienced," he said.

Randy soon learned that Madison's grandfather was named John. Madison gave him her grandmother Kathy's phone number, and Randy reached out to share his experience with her. During the call, Kathy asked Randy to describe what John looked like in the vision. Randy recalled, "I told her he had dark hair and maybe a light mustache." In response, Kathy sent him a photo of a young man in a military uniform, taken when John was in his early or late twenties. The moment Randy saw the picture, he recognized him and called Kathy back. "I said, Kathy, that's who I saw. There's no doubt about it. That's him."

Powerful Phone Call

Kathy shared with Randy that this wasn't the first time she had received a message from John. After his passing, she had been going through his belongings and came across a business card for someone at an insurance company. She wondered if John had a life insurance policy she hadn't known about, so she called the number on the card.

However, the man on the line informed her he was not the person named on the card, nor did he work at an insurance company. Surprised, Kathy double-checked the number, and the man pointed out that she had accidentally misdialed the area code. He explained that he was in California and then asked her where she was calling from. Kathy told him she was in Iowa and mentioned her name. As they spoke, she explained that her husband had recently passed away, and she had found this business card in his drawer, sparking a series of unexpected connections.

At this point in their conversation, the man shared something unusual that had happened to him. Four months prior, he explained, he had been in a severe motorcycle accident. Lying injured on the asphalt immediately afterward, he distinctly heard someone repeatedly shouting, "Tell Kathy from Iowa that John is okay." The man told Kathy that when the paramedics arrived on the scene, they found him alone and without a pulse. To him, it felt as though he had been sent back to deliver John's message, just as Randy had been.

7. The Question That Changed Everything

FRANCO ROMERO

She asked him, "How do you know this? Who told you because I haven't told anybody about certain things, and you know them clearly as though you were there?"

*

Franco Romero was born in Bogota, Colombia, and moved to the United States when he was eight months old. He had a near-death experience when he was just six months old. The memories of his NDE didn't resurface until he was 15, but when they did, they came back to him with vivid clarity. Franco began experiencing recurring dreams and visions of a hospital room filled with distressed, crying people. Most of the faces were unfamiliar, but he recognized his mother among them. In his dreams, everyone's focus was on a baby who appeared to be near death. Over time, these dreams intensified. They became more vivid, and Franco felt deeply connected to them as if he were the baby in distress.

When the dreams occurred nightly, Franco finally brought them up with his mother. "I had no idea that I had had a near-death experience until I brought up the subject to her as to whether it was it possible that I might've had a situation where

I has come close to dying in the past," he later recounted. He described the scenes he had been seeing in his dreams, sharing details he could not have known. He asked her, "Is it possible? Is it possible that any of this happened?" His mother's reaction was one of complete shock. She had never mentioned the incident to him, yet Franco's account mirrored exactly what had happened. His mother confirmed his dreams as memories from his near-death experience as a baby.

*

At six months old, Franco's mother grew concerned about his worsening chest cold and took him to the hospital. After an examination, the doctor recommended keeping him overnight for observation. As the hours went by, Franco's condition worsened significantly, and he was considered to be in critical danger. In his dreams Franco recalled experiencing a profound lightness as he floated above the hospital room, watching the people gathered around his small body below. He saw the look of worry on their faces and felt the intensity of their emotions as they feared for the fragile life in front of them.

As Franco's condition deteriorated, the doctor delivered grim news to his mother, explaining there was little hope and he might not survive the night. Instead of staying at his bedside, Franco's mother left the hospital and sought solace at a nearby church. In spirit form, Franco followed her closely as she made her way there. When she reached the altar, she prayed, but it was unlike a normal plea for divine intervention. Franco later recalled, "It was not your typical prayer of asking for God to save me, it was a prayer or what I described as a meditation, of gratitude, of appreciation that she had had, even though it was only six months, she had had such a beautiful, enriching experience with me, being my mother, that she was thankful for the little time that she had with me."

Franco sensed that, as his mother prayed in the quiet of the church, she experienced a powerful vision of him as a grown man. She saw not only that he would survive but glimpsed the person he would become, the kindness he would carry, the love he would share as a husband and father. Almost instantly, the energy in the church shifted and she felt a state of absolute serenity overcome her. She wasn't sure what had happened but knew no matter what, she was at peace with the outcome.

The second set of dreams saw Franco back in the hospital. This time, his focus was on a baby fighting for its life. He felt drawn toward the child, as if they were melding into one. Within moments, Franco sensed the baby's soul leaving its body. In that instant, he merged with its consciousness and found himself looking down at the scene below. He could see the people gathered there, praying for him.

The room went dark. When the light returned, Franco found himself floating above a desolate desert landscape, a group of weary people below. They appeared exhausted and hungry, their clothing worn and ragged. At first, he felt confused, noticing that the people gazed up in his direction. But he quickly realized they were looking past him, drawn to an intensely bright orb of light behind him. "When I turned around to look at it, it was probably five to ten sizes larger than our sun, and I remember thinking, why doesn't this hurt my eyes?" Each time he looked back down at the people, his focus shifted, drawn from one individual to another. First, he noticed an old man with outstretched hands and then a young boy with the same gesture. He sensed a connection between them, as if they were the same soul at different stages, reaching out with a unified longing. At first, he thought they might be reaching for him, as though they wanted to hold his hand. But he realized their outstretched arms were not meant for him. They were trying to touch the orb of light itself. Turning back, he saw the light had drawn closer, now almost directly above him.

An indescribable sensation overcame Franco, an unconditional love that far exceeded any earthly experience. Each cell in his body pulsated and reached toward the light with the same longing he had seen in the people below. It was as if every cell had a unique consciousness. "Every cell in my body had its own awareness and was reaching out to the light," Franco recalled, "I was feeling the experience of knowing myself as 50 trillion aspects of me." As the light descended, it enveloped Franco, immersing him in a state of pure ecstasy. He felt his form vibrating at an extraordinary rate as he moved deeper. Gradually, he realized that the light itself was composed of individual spiritual beings, each radiating an incredible brightness. They had a basic human form, but their faces and finer details remained indistinct. As Franco continued to gaze into this infinite expanse, he realized the light extended beyond any limits he could conceive. The spiritual beings within it seemed to merge into one unified presence, yet he could still sense each unique being within the whole.

Franco recalled focusing his attention on a particular being, far in the distance, yet feeling an instant, profound connection. "I knew them very intimately, and they knew me very intimately," he remembered. "It was as though I was them, and they were me." This sense of communion extended to every being in the vast light, yet he sensed that those closest to him shared an especially deep bond, as if they were more deeply connected with his soul. As he felt this feeling of unity, four of the beings moved toward him, radiating a sense of familiarity, love, and warmth that filled him with a sense of home. He recognized them on a soul level and felt reunited with his family. They formed a circle around him, completely enveloping him in their radiant glow. The experience he later described as his "million hugs."

The beings asked Franco a question that puzzled him: "What do you see?" Unsure of what they were asking, he initially replied that he saw an endless stream of beings. But the beings repeated the question, "What do you see?" Then, a realization struck him, he realized there was something vital he needed to understand about this space, a truth that would shape his life, his sense of self, and his relationship with what he later called God, Source, or Creator. The instant Franco had this revelation, he felt a presence, a gentle but firm touch on his right shoulder. "At that moment, I felt as though I was being told by a being, a collective presence of beings who had been guiding me through this experience, that my time there was ending." Despite his deep reluctance to leave, Franco suddenly moved rapidly through a tunnel, speeding away from the light and the beings he had connected to. The tunnel seemed to pull him forward with incredible force, and even though he had left the beings, the love and light he'd experienced remained with him.

Franco had the same dream repeatedly for months. Each time, he woke up drenched in sweat, feeling as if he had fallen back into his body after a terrifying plunge. It felt like a bad dream. "The dream was so, so real," he recalled. "Every time I woke up, I was almost in tears when I realized I was back in my bed. The crazy thing is, it didn't matter how many times I had this exact dream—I felt it like it had just happened for the first time." He was certain that the dream in the church and the one where he was surrounded by heavenly light were deeply connected. But he kept them to himself, fearing the worst. Franco knew something had happened to him as a baby, something beyond explanation. And no matter how much he tried to ignore it, the truth wouldn't fade. Reality, as he had always known it, was slipping away. He needed to talk to someone.

*

As Franco's mother made her way back to the hospital, she braced herself for the worst, assuming that she would find him either close to death or already gone. As she arrived, she noticed a crowd gathered near the entrance. Then, the doctor who had delivered the grim prognosis just hours earlier approached her. His eyes were filled with tears, but they weren't the tears of sorrow she had expected. Instead, they were tears of joy. He told her that something incredible had happened. Against all odds, Franco's vitals had suddenly stabilized. No one could explain how or why, but his body had recovered almost instantly. The expectation now was that he would make a full recovery. The next day, Franco was discharged from the hospital. The whole incident was written off as a medical miracle that would soon be forgotten.

Verification Events

Franco's mother

As Franco continued to experience his recurring dreams and visions, he eventually confided in his mother. He recounted his vivid memories, explaining how he'd felt himself out of his body, watching her from above during that night in the hospital. He described, in detail, her journey to the church, sharing the precise words and feelings in her prayers. "You weren't asking for me to survive," he told her. "Your prayers were filled with gratitude and appreciation for the chance to be with me, even if it was just for six months."

Franco described something even more profound: the moment in the church when her energy shifted. He explained a peaceful vision, where she saw him as he would be in the future, a grown man, the person he would become, the love he would share, and the family he might have.

"I was explaining all of this to her, and her mouth just opened like she was speechless," Franco recalled. "It was obvious that I had hit a chord with her, that she was stunned that I knew first and foremost that this event had even happened. Then that it was recalled in a very specific, very clear manner." These were events that his mother had not shared with anyone. She asked him, puzzled, "How do you know this? Who told you because I haven't told anybody about certain things, and you know them clearly as though you were there?"

*

Franco had no logical explanation for what he had seen, only that the details had come to him vividly in his dreams. His mother urged him to share his incredible story, but he refused. "My brother had had some very intense experiences in a home that was possessed and when he decided to talk about them, it didn't bode well for him. As such, I vowed to keep my story to myself. Little did I know that destiny had different plans for me which would later reunite me with even more remembrances of what transpired while I was in the Light."

Over the following decades, Franco experienced a series of massive downloads that reshaped his life forever. Without realizing it, he was on a path toward becoming a clairvoyant, a shamanic master and teacher of all things related to consciousness. These memories would serve him well as he began sharing his story with hundreds of thousands of people—those eager to understand what truly lies beyond this world and how it all connects to the powerful awakening of humanity now unfolding.

8. A Soul's Surrender and a Life Reclaimed

MALCOLM NAIR

I told each and every person what they had thought of me and what they said to everybody on their phone calls." Malcolm recalls, "They didn't know how to react to this. They said that I was correct, and they would say, 'That's true. How do you know that?' They didn't know what to say."

*

Malcolm grew up hearing one thing over and over: "You weren't supposed to be born." His story, however, wasn't one of hope and miracles like the tales of children born against the odds. Instead, it was a story marked by abuse, pain, and hardship from the very start. His mother was trapped in an abusive relationship with his father, who, in his violence, tried to end Malcolm's life before he was even born. Unable to cope with the abuse, his mother did things she hoped would cause a miscarriage. But despite all of that, Malcolm was born, and when he was just one-year-old, his parents separated. As a child, he grew up in an environment filled with chaos and fear. Raised in low-income housing, his stepfather struggled with drug addiction and his mother struggled with narcissistic men and she became jealous and insecure. By the time he was eight, his stepfather and his peers had introduced him to marijuana, cigarettes, and alcohol. In response to the trauma, Malcolm acted out with violence and self-loathing, pushing others away. This led to broken relationships and deep insecurity.

Looking back on that time, Malcolm said, "I had no self-control. I was destructive. I was very abusive. I didn't know how to love or appreciate. I didn't know how to build relationships or respect for one another." Without the proper guidance or support, Malcolm struggled to form healthy relationships or set boundaries. Instead, he mirrored the harmful behaviors he had witnessed. By the age of fourteen, Malcolm had fallen into a crack cocaine addiction. Between the ages of 15 and 17 he was homeless and at 17 he impregnated his girlfriend with their first child.

On the night of his near-death experience, Malcolm was at a party where drugs flowed freely. Throughout the night, he mixed alcohol with cocaine, mushrooms, and marijuana. At 2:00 a.m., Malcolm left the party and got into his car, planning to drive to a friend's house. Despite already being heavily intoxicated, he continued to consume drugs as he drove through town. "I had a whole bag of mushrooms," he recalled. "I don't know how much was in there, maybe 10 to 20 grams of mushrooms, and I was munching on it like it was a snack. Every time, I'd just pinch some with my thumb and two fingers and put it in my mouth and I was smoking marijuana." Malcolm felt lost and paranoid. He was speeding through the streets, the effects of the drugs overwhelming his senses. Flashing lights disoriented him as he drifted in and out of a hallucinatory daze, and he lost control of the car. "I sideswiped two vehicles and just smashed my head into the windshield," Malcolm recalled. "I'd kind of doze off and come back to consciousness, then I'd hit the gas harder. Eventually, I went up someone's lawn and hit a house, going 100 kilometers an hour.

Everything became still and silent. He could not move and felt powerless. As the gravity of his situation set in, Malcolm gave up any hope of survival, and in that moment of surrender, he felt his spirit lift from his body. Malcolm stood by the wreckage, watching the chaos unfold around him. He saw the shocked homeowners emerge from their house to assess the damage. The car had crashed into their son's bedroom and in the impact Malcolm was thrown into the passenger side of the car. By some stroke of luck, the room was empty. Soon, police cars and an ambulance appeared on the scene.

"I didn't know what to do," Malcolm recalled. "I wasn't in tune with any vision or insight at that time." He watched as the EMTs extracted his body from the wreckage and placed him in the ambulance, trying to resuscitate him. In this out-of-body state, Malcolm found he could tune into the thoughts and feelings of the EMTs. He could hear them discussing his condition, remarking on how he was losing too much blood. As the ambulance sped away, Malcolm discovered he could move in and out of his body at will. Inside the vehicle, he would watch the EMTs working over him, feeling their dedication and urgency. Then, shifting outside, he would observe the ambulance moving down the highway from a detached point of view. This back-and-forth continued as he rode between life and death.

When they arrived at the hospital, Malcolm followed as staff rushed his body through the hallways. "They're pulling and rushing me into a room, you know, the ICU," he recalled. As he observed himself being taken in and out of surgery, he felt both present and distant, watching as specialists, doctors, and nurses moved around him in a coordinated effort to keep him alive. Malcolm found himself attuned to the thoughts and emotions of everyone around him. "I can hear whispers, and I can hear people's thoughts," he said. The quiet comments of the staff reached him. Some murmured, "My God, look at him," while others looked on in silent shock. Malcolm felt their concern, their disbelief, and even the faint glimmer of hope some held for his survival. To give his body much needed strength he entered it, and despite the physical trauma, he removed his neck brace and breathing tube.

The injuries were severe and extensive. One of his eyes had suffered 75% nerve damage, he had paralysis affecting over 75% of his body, and there was considerable brain damage. As his family arrived at the hospital, Malcolm observed them from his out-of-body perspective, watching their conversations and the flurry of calls they made. "My family is from Fiji," he explained, "and, you know, they're calling Australia and New Zealand, reaching out to people who couldn't be there, and calling aunts and uncles to either come or just giving them the warnings and telling them what's going on."

Malcolm could feel the waves of emotion coming from his family: fear, grief, and the urge to reach out and connect with loved ones. He explored the hospital, moving freely through the building, observing patients as they ate, watching the staff at the front desk, and drifting through different rooms. He found his mother on a phone call with his uncle. Malcolm discovered he could listen in not only to her words but on her thoughts before she even spoke. "I can hear her thoughts before she says them while the phone was ringing," he recalled. When his uncle picked up, Malcolm tuned into their conversation from both sides.

"I was able to tune in and go into that frequency," he explained, "to tune in to him receiving that signal. I could hear his thoughts, what he was saying, and how he interacted with his family. I was able to be with both of them simultaneously." Malcolm saw his uncle as he drove his family enroute to a vacation in California. When they received the news about the accident, his uncle immediately turned the car around, explaining that they needed to go to the hospital. Malcolm watched his cousins' reactions. He saw their disappointment and frustration. They didn't want to change their plans and suggested they shouldn't visit him at all, insisting they should continue on to California.

As Malcolm's condition worsened, his mother faced an agonizing decision. The doctors explained that there were faint signs of life in his body, but there was no certainty about his chances of survival. They asked her if they should switch off the life support. With a heavy heart, she made the painful choice to disconnect the equipment. Though she still hoped for a miracle, she prepared herself for the worst.

The instant the machines were disconnected, Malcolm felt pulled away. He felt the transition, as the last link to his body, was broken. He drifted effortlessly through the hospital, passing through walls and up through every floor until he floated outside the building. Before long, he found himself high above the Earth, looking down on it from beyond the atmosphere. "And I'm like, now what?" He sensed a decision pressing upon him but quickly realized it wasn't one he could control in the way he was used to. "I had to release the self-control that we all have," he reflected. At that moment of surrender, a powerful force pulled him into a swirling vortex.

As he traveled through this vortex, he witnessed many energy patterns, frequencies, and glimpses of other dimensions. It was as if he were moving through the fabric of existence itself, experiencing layers of reality and understanding in ways that were beyond human comprehension. Finally, Malcolm found himself in a vast, seemingly endless darkness. "I ended up seeing black. I was getting nervous," he recalled. "I was in the unknown. I was a little bit nervous and a little worried." As he drifted into this dark void, he wondered if he would ever see light again. Malcolm surrendered completely. He released his fears, giving himself over fully to the darkness. "I just surrendered. I just gave in; I completely gave in."

A powerful white light appeared, illuminating the surrounding space. But this was not just a simple light. "It's not like a white light," he explained. "It's like a supernova. A great expansion." This light was more than brightness; it was 'source light,' a vast, pulsating energy filled with pure awareness. The light felt alive, carrying with it intelligence and peace, as if he were standing in the presence of the very essence of creation itself. Malcolm sensed he had arrived at a place beyond the limits of his understanding. As he stood in the source of light, waves of overwhelming emotions flooded him: compassion, forgiveness, and a complete absence of judgment. In this place, he felt the light accepted and understood every part of him, including his past mistakes and struggles.

Spiritual beings and angels surrounded him, woven into a vast, interconnected web of pure love. They existed in what Malcolm described as "the safe haven of love and harmony and appreciation and respect and compassion." Here, he felt a deep, sacred unity, as if each being was part of a harmonious whole connected by endless love.

An incredible white light offered a welcoming presence of love. "But I feel that it was me," he said. "I looked at my life review and, in a flash, in an instant, it wasn't me being out of my body anymore and being able to travel here and there. I was able just to see the timeline of that life that I lived. I could see the emotions and hear how their hearts were in all the people I'd ever encountered. All the people who have helped me and I've let down, and I used, and I've abused, and I've turned an eye to, and I've just brushed under the carpet and everything and in my life and family, friends, and acquaintances that have brushed things under the carpet and all the emotions that I wanted to resurface. I'm telling you just everything beyond what I'm saying. I´ve seen it all and I just could not accept that. It wasn't egotistical. It was almost shame. I felt guilt and shame. Like, why couldn't I make a better decision? Why couldn't I say I'm sorry to a woman? Why can't I say I'm sorry to a father or a brother or a man? How come I didn't know how to build a relationship with a man or a woman or how to be like a child or be childlike or love a child or know how to raise a kid or know how to be respectful to an employer? I was ashamed of myself."

Malcolm wanted to return to his body. Yet, he realized it wasn't his physical mind craving the return; it was his soul, driven by a deeper purpose. In response, a voice asked him, "Are you sure?" Malcolm's answer was clear. "Yeah, I'm sure." At that moment, the spiritual beings around him bowed their heads in a gesture of compassion and respect, honoring his choice. He fell backward into the darkness, drifting away from the haven he had experienced. The journey back felt long, like going across an infinite expanse. But then, in a sudden, jarring moment, Malcolm found himself reconnected with his body.

"I ended up waking up about 10 to 15 minutes later, when everybody was settled down and kind of waiting for me to wake up because they had my heartbeat going," Malcolm recalled.

Within three days, Malcolm's lungs had fully recovered, and his bone fusion was advancing at an impressive pace. While he remained conscious of his body's healing process, the medical team continued to monitor his condition with regular assessments. After six days in hospital, he was discharged, having achieved a remarkable and complete recovery. The doctors remarked that they had never encountered a case as severe as his, where the bone and lung injuries healed so quickly. They stated, "You shouldn't be alive."

Verification Events

After his return, Malcolm shared with his family the vivid experiences he had during his time in the hospital.

Thoughts and conversations

"When I woke up from my life support, I told each and every person what they had thought of me and what they said to everybody on their phone calls." Malcolm recalls, "They didn't know how to react to this. They said that I was correct, and they would say, 'That's true. How do you know that?' they didn't know what to say." Malcolm shared with his mother exactly what she had said to his uncle during their phone call. Her reaction was one of shock and disbelief. "What? How do you know that? How did you know that? Only I know that," she asked, astonished by his accurate recall.

Malcolm recounted interactions he'd had with family members, his sisters, stepsisters, and others who had come into the room and whispered things to him, offering words of comfort or sharing news about other family members. He even told them the specific prayers they had spoken, repeating their words verbatim. The family members were stunned, left "stone-cold shocked" by his accurate recounting of their private thoughts and words. Malcolm's ability to describe these moments so precisely left them speechless.

Malcolm recounted the specific struggles they had been experiencing. He shared with his sister exactly what she had been thinking and feeling during those tense moments, leaving her completely speechless.

Even now, Malcolm continues to sense people's thoughts, feelings, and emotions, a sensitivity he still carries with him. "I still do it," he explained. What struck him most was how people seemed unable to believe such awareness was natural. "That's what bugged me out," he reflected, "the fact that they were still living their lives, not trying to listen to the awareness, to see that these truths are possible."

9. To What Degree Have You Loved?

JEFF OLSEN

Dr. Jeff O'Driscoll and nurse Rachel, both part of the trauma team, also saw Tamara's spirit in the room.

*

On March 31, 1997, Jeff Olsen, his wife Tamara, and their two children, Griffin and Spencer, set off on their drive home after a wonderful Easter weekend spent with Tamara's parents in St. George, Southern Utah. After their goodbyes, Jeff and Tamara sat in the front seats of the car while their children were in the back. The drive home would take several hours, and after merging onto the interstate, they settled in for the long journey. Jeff set the cruise control at 75 miles per hour, taking Tamara's hand while she slept beside him.

Jeff doesn't remember exactly what caused the accident. He may have dozed off, or perhaps it was a sudden gust of crosswind. "It's sometimes difficult to talk about," he recalled, "but I lost control of the car, and it rolled down the road. I blacked out for a lot of that." The vehicle tumbled violently out of control, rolling seven or eight times before coming to a stop.

When Jeff regained consciousness, his orientation was unclear to him. He simply knew he could not move and felt pinned down. "I was either pinned to the floorboard or the seat. I'm not sure," he said.

In the moments that followed, he could hear his seven-year-old son, Spencer, crying in the back seat. "As a father, that was a relief," he said, knowing at least one of his children was alive. Jeff tried to reach his son, but he quickly realized he was pinned down and unable to move, feeling intense pain. He struggled to breathe, still unaware of the full extent of his injuries. "My back had been damaged. My rib cage had been damaged. My lungs were collapsing," he explained. "My right arm had almost been torn off, and the seat belt had cut through me, rupturing my intestines and ripping my abdomen wide open."

As Spencer continued to cry in the back seat, Jeff realized he couldn't hear Griffin or Tamara at all. Slowly, the truth dawned on him. Both his wife and youngest son had died in the crash. Panic gripped him as he lay trapped, knowing his surviving child needed him but feeling powerless to reach him. Jeff drifted into unconsciousness, fading into darkness. "It was in that darkness that I felt light come," he later recalled. "When I say that, it felt like light literally came and encircled me, and it comforted me." At that moment, a sense of calm and warmth surrounded him, and he felt he was rising above the accident scene.

As the light enveloped him, Jeff felt an overwhelming wave of unconditional love wash over him, dissolving all his pain and fear. He was transported to a place filled with joy, a realm that felt deeply familiar, as if he had always belonged there. With his eyes closed, he took a deep, pain-free breath. He felt a gentle touch. Opening his eyes, he saw his wife, Tamara, standing before him in the light, free from any trace of the trauma she had suffered in the crash. "My wife, who I knew was deceased at the scene, was there in the light with me, and she was absolutely gorgeous," Jeff recalled. Tamara spoke softly, telling him, "Jeff, you can't come. You can't come. You've got to go back." He understood he still had a purpose to fulfill, a life to return to. He thought of Spencer, his young son, crying in the back seat, and the pull of love and responsibility grew stronger. As the light faded he lost consciousness, feeling the weight and pain of his body.

Miraculously, his seven-year-old son, Spencer, had walked away from the accident with a broken arm and bruised ribs. Later, Jeff learned that a doctor had been in a car close to the accident scene, and he had provided immediate help until the EMTs arrived. Jeff remained unconscious as rescuers worked carefully to free him from the wreckage. Once they had safely removed him, an emergency helicopter airlifted him to a trauma center in the nearest city.

Consciousness gradually returned, and in spirit form he drifted through the bustling trauma center. He watched the staff at work, yet no one could see him. This out-of-body experience brought him an astonishing level of connection.

"I was completely aware of the patients, the doctors, the nurses, and the families of the patients," he recalled. "It was like I was connected. I knew their hearts, their love, their pain, their motivations, their sorrows. I knew it all, as if it was a part of me. There was this absolute connection, this oneness, which was just infused with unconditional love." The insights Jeff received in this state revealed a truth he hadn't known before. Each person, from the heroin addict to the saintly grandmother, was inherently glorious. Every individual, regardless of their life's struggles or triumphs, was an extraordinary being at their core.

As he floated past a nurse, he became instantly aware of her entire life, experiencing her emotions and memories as if they were his own. He felt the pain of the abuse she had endured as a child. Yet, in the same moment, he saw her as a radiant, kindhearted soul, a magnificent being whose trials had transformed her into someone capable of profound healing and empathy. In awe, he thought, "Wow, you mean that abuse transformed you into this benevolent, noble, and compassionate nurse who is literally healing people in the hospital?"

As Jeff journeyed through the hospital, he noticed a divine presence accompanying him, as if a gentle yet powerful voice was speaking just behind him. This presence conveyed wisdom, guiding him in a new way of seeing through the eyes of pure love. The divine voice asked him a question that resonated deeply: "To what degree have you learned to love?" This question carried a significance that reached beyond anything he had known. It wasn't about accomplishments, accolades, or beliefs; it was about the depth of his heart and the love he had shared with others. This question invited Jeff to reflect on his own journey, challenging him to see life through the lens of compassion and to recognize that love, more than anything else, was the ultimate purpose and measure of a life well lived.

Eventually, he came upon a gurney holding a body in critical condition, badly injured, barely alive, and seemingly on the brink of death. As he looked at it, he noticed a striking difference. The profound sense of connection and oneness he'd felt with everyone else he encountered was missing. He stepped closer, and in a moment of clarity, he realized the battered body before him was his own. A complex mix of emotions flooded him. He felt deep sadness at the sight of his lifeless, broken form, but also a sense of awe at the resilience and miraculous nature of the human body. The moment Jeff recognized the body as his, he knew he needed to go back. In an instant, he found himself reunited with the weight and reality of physical existence. "It felt like I was in a lead cocoon," he described, "but it was coupled with all the guilt, grief, remorse, trauma, and pain that I had been free of while out of the body."

In the trauma room, the medical team worked to stabilize Jeff and bring him back from the brink. Dr. Jeff O'Driscoll, one of the center's level one trauma physicians, was attending to another patient when a nurse urgently approached him. She told him she had witnessed something extraordinary and insisted he come to the trauma room immediately. As they walked, she explained she had felt and seen Jeff's deceased wife, Tamara.

When Dr. O'Driscoll and the nurse entered the trauma room, a scene greeted them unlike any they had encountered before. Above Jeff's body, Tamara's soul hovered, her presence observing as the medical team worked frantically to save her husband's life. As Dr. O'Driscoll watched, he felt Tamara communicate with him telepathically, expressing her deep gratitude for everything they were doing to help. At that moment, Jeff, still in an in-between state, looked across the room and caught Dr. O'Driscoll's eye. The doctor gave him a quiet, understanding nod, as if to confirm something unspoken.

As the days passed, Jeff was overcome with a deep, consuming grief over the loss of his young son, Griffin. The pain weighed heavily on him, and his sorrow grew with each passing day. Finally, after his abdominal wounds had stabilized, he reached a point where he could roll onto his side. That night, for the first time in weeks, he drifted into a deep, restful sleep. Jeff felt himself lifting above his body, rising into the familiar light.

The light gradually faded, like a lifting fog, to reveal a breathtaking place filled with love, peace, and beauty. Free from the confines of pain, he found himself able to jump and run. Despite the freedom he felt, Jeff instinctively understood that his visit here was temporary. To his left, he noticed a corridor extending into the distance, and he felt a pull to follow it. At the end of the incredibly long corridor, he came upon a crib. In it lay Griffin, peacefully asleep.

"I went and picked up my son," Jeff recalled. "I couldn't even speak of this for years. I would just cry. But I picked up my little boy, and I could feel him, solid against me." In that sacred moment, he felt Griffin's warm breath on his neck and the familiar scent of his hair, filling him with a sense of peace and gratitude. "I'm just like, it's my little boy. He's okay, and I'm here, getting to say goodbye to him, too." As he held Griffin close, savoring every detail, Jeff noticed a presence behind him. It was an overwhelming presence, wise, vast, and cosmic, filling the space with an overwhelming sense of love and wholeness.

Having been raised in a conservative Christian home, Jeff felt a wave of fear wash over him. "I thought, if this powerful force behind me is God, I'm probably in big trouble," he remembered. The weight of guilt pressed on him. He feared that his son's life had been cut short because of his own actions in causing the accident.

A sense of unworthiness filled him as he thought, "I don't dare turn around. I hope there's some way I can be forgiven." Yet, before he could finish that thought, something extraordinary happened. "I can't even explain what it felt like or what happened," Jeff said, "but as soon as I thought that, it felt like those divine arms just wrapped around both me and my son." He felt himself and Griffin being held in an embrace so infused with love that it melted his fears and guilt.

"Suddenly, the lid just came off," he described, "and there was this huge download of peace and love."

As Jeff felt God's embrace, his life played out before him. Every passing moment showed the impact of his actions on everyone he had known. He didn't just watch the events unfold; he experienced them. The emotions of others poured over him, and he felt their happiness, sadness, and pain as if they were his own. When Jeff saw the mistakes he had made and the pain he had caused, a deep regret washed over him. The weight of those moments filled him with self-judgment, and he longed for forgiveness.

Amid these thoughts, a voice broke through. It reminded Jeff of a simple truth: the only one judging him was himself. God wasn't there to condemn him. Instead, God reassured him that he was deeply loved and cherished. Jeff realized he was just as precious as the child he held in his arms.

Then came a moment, a chance for Jeff to release his son into God's care. Deep down, Jeff knew that entrusting Griffin to God was the most loving and peaceful choice he could make. He gently laid his son in the crib. In that instant, everything changed, and something suddenly pulled him back into his body. The comfort and light disappeared, replaced by the sharp pain and darkness of the hospital bed.

After some weeks, medical staff moved Jeff from the ICU to a surgical recovery room. One afternoon, he received two visitors, a man and a woman he didn't recognize. Assuming they were a couple, their presence puzzled Jeff, unsure why unfamiliar people would visit him. They introduced themselves as Dr. Jeff O'Driscoll and Rachel, a trauma team nurse who had helped during his emergency care. Jeff thanked them sincerely for their work, and Rachel brought a chair close to his bed. As she sat down, Rachel's eyes filled with tears, and she reached for tissues from Jeff's bedside stand. "She started to cry," Jeff recalled. "She said, 'We must tell you why we came.'"

Rachel explained that both she and Dr. O'Driscoll had seen Tamara's spirit hovering over his bed as Jeff received life-saving treatment. Hearing this, Jeff felt a rush of emotion. "I began to weep because I had this profound, out-of-body, near-death experience. My wife was so near, and the fact that this nurse saw something and experienced something and was willing to share it was really powerful for me."

Rachel and Dr. O'Driscoll told him that Tamara's spirit had expressed her gratitude, thanking them for everything they were doing to save Jeff's life. "I thought that's exactly what she would do. That's her heart," Jeff explained.

*

Dr. O'Driscoll wrote about this experience in his book 'Not Yet: Near-Life Experiences & Lessons Learned.'

Late in my shift on March 31, 1997, Rachel grabbed me by the arm. She was a perpetually calm nurse, now with an urgent expression. It sounds odd to non-ER people, but ER people seldom walk or talk with an outward appearance of urgency. They may feel it, but they seldom show it. Too much urgency in an ER makes people nervous. Despite the often-urgent needs of patients, ER people tend to move in a calm, deliberate manner. So, Rachel's tone caught my attention. "She's here," she said. "You've got to come to the trauma room."

"Who's here?" I asked. "What are you talking about?"

"His wife. She's here."

Rachel had been in the trauma suite and seen him arrive. Now, she was tugging on my arm.

"She's there," she said. "C'mon."

I finally gave way to her insistence as I realized what she was saying. Prior conversations in more relaxed circumstances had primed me for her assertions. She'd experienced numerous spiritual phenomena in the past. Some of her experiences, as she'd shared them privately, had brought me to tears. I'd had my own experiences. We'd discussed some at length.

In the trauma suite, I saw the usual army of professionals surrounding a gurney. Bits of an unconscious and battered body were visible through the cracks between personnel. I saw the usual flurry of activity and heard the hum of voices: vital signs, the tail end of a report from the transport team, orders, acknowledgments, and tentative plans. Almost as quickly, however, the sounds all faded into silence, like a television show with the sound turned off. People's lips still moved—they could still hear one another—but the room fell silent for me. Even Rachel's voice was gone. A tingle—almost a vibration—began in the center of my soul and radiated outward to the tip of each digit. I felt the hair on my arms and neck stand at attention.

The treatment area was large, with an elevated ceiling and a mirrored observation room that looked down on the scene for teaching purposes. Tamara stood high above my right shoulder and about ten feet away, about halfway between Jeff and I. We'd never met, but I knew her. She calmly surveyed the room, sometimes looking toward me, sometimes toward her severely injured spouse. She had a pleasant countenance and a warm, welcoming disposition. She had long, wavy, blonde hair.

I walked to the gurney and looked at Jeff for the first time. I looked at his badly injured legs. People moved around me, all doing their respective tasks. I had no tasks. I was free to take in the experience, keenly aware of Tamara's continued surveillance over my right shoulder. I may have felt for a pulse in Jeff's left foot; I don't remember for sure.

I don't recall what Tamara said to me in the trauma suite, looking down from her elevated position. Though facing toward Jeff, I could see her behind me. I could see her as clearly behind me as I could see him in front. I could see in every direction at the same time and take it all in more efficiently than if I'd been focusing on a single spot. It's been more than twenty years, and I've rarely spoken of it, but I remember that part clearly. Tamara may not have said anything at all. Whether she spoke through the silence or communicated without words, I remember quite clearly her expressions of pure gratitude. She was grateful for the team and all they were doing. She was grateful to me for being aware of her. My overall impression was that she was a grateful person and would express her appreciation to each individual if she were able to do so. At that moment, to borrow a phrase I would later hear Jeff use, I knew her heart.

*

Jeff spent five months in hospital and underwent 18 surgeries during his recovery. It took nearly a year before he could function normally again.

Verification Event

As Jeff lay in the trauma center, his deceased wife, Tamara, appeared to him. Dr. Jeff O'Driscoll and nurse Rachel, both part of the trauma team, also saw Tamara's spirit in the room. She floated above Jeff's bed, visible to all three of them, confirming the experience Jeff was having.

Tamara's Dream

An eerie premonition from Tamara lingered with Jeff. The night before they set off on their journey to Utah, she had a vivid dream. In it, she saw Jeff marrying another woman. When she told him about the dream, she explained that, strangely, while watching this wedding unfold, she felt a deep sense of peace and contentment. "Keep in mind, this is before the accident, and we're a couple that's madly in love," Jeff explained, reflecting on the unusual serenity she'd felt in what should have been an unsettling vision. In hindsight, Tamara's dream seemed to carry an otherworldly message, almost as if she sensed, on some level, what was to come. Her peace in the dream provided Jeff with an unexpected layer of comfort later on.

Reference

Jeff Olsen, (2018) *'Knowing: Memoirs of a journey beyond the veil and choosing joy after tragic loss'*, Envoy Publishing

Dr. O'Driscoll, (2017) *'Not Yet: Near-Life Experiences & Lessons Learned'*, Jeff's Publishing Company

10. Corinna's Warning: A Life Unfinished

LYNDA CRAMER

The sheriff, visibly shocked, asked, "How do you know I asked him all those questions?"

She replied, "Because I was in that living room, near the ceiling, watching you asking him the questions."

*

In May 2001, Lynda Cramer, a 35-year-old woman from Australia, was living in North Carolina with her husband, Sam. They had been married for just a year. As an Australian citizen, Lynda needed to submit her immigration paperwork so she could legally stay in the United States. Sam didn't feel the paperwork was important. He believed Lynda should simply stay in the U.S. without legal status, which led to disagreements between them. These differences of opinion grew over time, and the tension between them escalated into episodes of domestic violence.

On May 6th, Lynda came down with a chest infection and went to bed early to rest. But at around 2 a.m., she awoke, struggling to breathe and feeling an urgent need to use the toilet. "I woke up, and I couldn't breathe. It was horrendous," she recalled. "It took me about ten minutes just to get to the bathroom."

Lynda made it to the bathroom, collapsed on the toilet, and fought to stay awake. Shortly after, Sam entered and found her lifeless, her skin a pale blue. He later said he had heard her calling out to him and banging on the wall, though Lynda herself had no memory of this. Panicked, Sam laid her on the floor and called 911. The emergency operator guided him through CPR as he waited for the ambulance to arrive. "I've now got my one hundred and sixty-eight page medical file from the hospital," Lynda stated. "In there, it says that when the ambulance arrived at the house, I was unresponsive. No heart rate, no breathing, clinically dead for at least 14 minutes."

While Sam was performing CPR, Lynda found herself conscious and floating near the ceiling of their living room, viewing the scene below. She felt weightless, as though gravity no longer had any hold on her, and looking down at herself, she noticed her legs faded away below the knees. Strangely, her night clothes appeared pristine, as though they were brand new, and her hands looked much younger, free of the usual signs of age. Lynda's experience of floating above the room felt completely natural.

Two paramedics came through the front door and went directly to the bathroom. "The first people I saw coming in were the two paramedics," Lynda recalled clearly. "I can still see what those two people looked like." One paramedic was young, in his early twenties, while the other was older, probably in his forties. The older man was thin and carried two medical bags as he hurried into the house.

Next, three more uniformed people entered the house. They began discussing what was happening, unaware of Lynda's presence. Sam also joined them and answered questions about the situation. Despite her attempts to speak to them, Lynda quickly realized she could not make a sound.

Her perception, however, was sharper than ever. She could clearly read the name tags on their uniforms and hear every word spoken. Describing the sheriff, she recalled, "I saw the nameplate on his badge. I noticed he had a gun on his belt and a walkie-talkie behind it. Then he went out to the car and came back with a clipboard." The sheriff asked Sam questions, taking notes on the clipboard. "He was asking questions like, 'Have you two been fighting lately? Are there any children in the house? Does she have any physical signs of abuse that you've inflicted on her?'" Lynda listened closely to every word, paying attention to the sheriff's serious tone.

The paramedics ran out to the ambulance, quickly returned, and headed into the bathroom. A few minutes later, Lynda watched as they emerged with her body on a trolley. An oxygen bottle was next to her, and an oxygen mask covered her mouth and nose. They wheeled her out of the house, the men in uniform following closely behind with Sam.

After they put Lynda's body in the ambulance, she watched Sam return to the house. He moved quickly, collecting his wallet and keys, which he had apparently left in the bedroom. "So my ex-husband was the last one out the door," she noted. "He must have left his wallet and his keys in the bedroom. Now, this is after my body left the building. My body was on the gurney in the back of the ambulance by now."

Left alone in the dark, quiet room, Lynda waited in silence, taking in the surrounding stillness. Thirty seconds later, the door unexpectedly opened, and a collection of dark blue orbs of light drifted in. The blue of these orbs was unlike anything she had seen on earth, intensely vivid, a dark blue fluorescent glitter with a mesmerizing radiance. Each orb had a bright white light at its center. They varied in size, some small and others quite large, all floating around the room without ever colliding. Lynda sensed these orbs were more than just lights. They felt intelligent, almost sentient, as if each one was observing her with curiosity. They drew close, moving around her purposefully, and it appeared they were communicating in their silent movements. Then, just as suddenly as they had entered, the orbs moved toward the door in unison, leaving the room with a graceful, synchronized exit, and the door closed behind them.

After a few seconds alone in the dark room, Lynda transitioned into an unfamiliar space, which she described as the "fog stage." This new space had no shape, light, or any other details. It was simply an empty, featureless expanse, leaving her with no real perception of anything around her.

Yet, as quickly as she entered this fog, she found herself in another setting.

Lynda explained the transition as immediate, saying, "If you just close your eyes, and when you open them, you're in a totally different location. But you don't feel yourself move. There's no momentum." She likened it to sitting in a familiar room, observing everything, then closing her eyes briefly and on opening them to find herself on top of Mount Everest, surrounded by ice and snow, wondering, "How the heck did I get here?" That, she said, was the fog stage.

Lynda was in a breathtaking landscape. Vibrant flowers bloomed around her, and tall trees stretched high above her. In the distance, towering mountains rose against the backdrop of an otherworldly sky, with buildings scattered throughout the scene. These structures radiated energy, and it felt as though they were capable of emotions as if they were beings in their own right.

Everything around her, the flowers, the grass, the trees, emitted a powerful, harmonious energy. The colors were unlike anything she had ever seen before. "I can close my eyes now tonight, and I can still see the flowers. I can still see the colors," Lynda explained. "Here on Earth, we only use about 5% of the color spectrum. So it's very hard for me to explain these colors."

Lynda realized that in this place, her perception stretched far beyond what was possible on Earth. She struggled to find the right words to describe it, but there was a deep, intuitive understanding of everything around her. It was as if the entire realm spoke to her, and she understood it all.

Music filled the air, though it seemed to come from no single source. Instead, the trees, flowers, and even the air seemed to create the music. It was a harmonious melody, impossible to tire of, and it felt as though the music was a fundamental part of this world, existing in every living thing.

Many people existed in this space. They seemed to be aware of her but paid little attention to her. "There were hundreds of people that I saw," she recalled. "They weren't too interested in me. It was like they knew I wasn't staying."

What caught her attention was how these individuals could change their appearance in an instant with nothing more than a thought. Their clothing changed into any style or color they wanted, and their hair could grow longer or become shorter. It was as if their appearance was a direct reflection of their inner thoughts.

Although Lynda felt she had spent months exploring the incredible landscape, it seemed as if she had only seen a tiny part of it. "I was traveling around in this area, going into buildings, exploring different places, up and down mountains," she recalled. Here, movement wasn't bound by time or physical effort; it was driven purely by thought. With just a single intention, she found herself instantly transported. "You can just move yourself there in one thought," she explained. "You're instantly projected to be on that mountain range just because you want to be there."

Lynda felt a presence behind her to the left, and when she turned, she saw a woman who felt immediately familiar as if she had been with Lynda her entire life. There were no words spoken between them; they communicated telepathically. The woman told Lynda she needed to hurry.

Before Lynda could say anything, the woman transported her into the fog stage. When the fog cleared, she stood outside an enormous structure. It resembled a cathedral, but it was much larger and grander than anything Lynda had seen on Earth. The building radiated its own energy, and the stained-glass windows were vibrant with color. Each one reached one hundred feet toward the ceiling, filled with a unique energy of its own. As she took in the surroundings, Lynda marveled at the soaring ceiling above her. It felt like there was something important within the building, something she was meant to discover.

As Lynda approached the building, she noticed three beings of light waiting for her at its entrance. They had no discernable facial features or recognizable form, and she wasn't sure if they were even human. The being in the center stood twelve feet tall, while the two on either side were about ten feet tall. Each of their heads radiated a light that reminded Lynda of the blue orbs she had seen earlier in her house, but was far more vibrant. The surrounding beings radiated an incredibly bright light, but Lynda felt no discomfort looking at them. Their presence filled the space with an overwhelming sense of love, something she could feel as if the love was vibrating within her.

One being approached Lynda and asked, "Are you prepared?" She answered, "Yes." In that instant, a box appeared in front of her. When it opened, Lynda saw every moment of her life captured within it. She realized she could reach into the box, choose any memory, and watch it unfold in her hand.

Then, the being spoke again, saying, "You are not here to judge."

At that moment, Lynda understood she wasn't just going to relive her memories; she was about to experience them from the perspective of the people she had interacted with. She would feel the emotions she had caused in others, both the joy and the pain. As she experienced each moment, Lynda realized how far-reaching her actions were. Each emotion, each interaction, had ripples that extended outward, affecting not just the people involved but the lives of those they encountered afterward. Lynda felt the full impact of even the smallest moments.

As she watched, Lynda judged herself, deeply feeling the consequences of her actions and seeing her impact on others. Yet the beings of light surrounding her offered no judgment. They waited, compassionately allowing her to complete her journey.

Without warning, Lynda found herself transported back to the fog stage, only to quickly be thrust into an endless, white, featureless space.

A woman approached from about fifty feet away. She wore a simple dress with no jewelry or makeup, and her face showed clear signs of agitation. She demanded, "What are you doing here?" Immediately, Lynda felt this encounter differed from the others she had experienced. Unlike the beings of light, this woman seemed tense and angry, and she spoke to Lynda with her voice, not telepathically. "Why are you here?" the woman repeated, "Don't you know you're not supposed to be here yet?" Lynda felt something was wrong.

The woman said, "Look, my name is Corinna. I know you because we are related." Lynda admitted, "I don't know where I am." Corinna replied, "You aren't supposed to be here. You've got to go back and finish it." Lynda asked, "Finish what?"

The question seemed to make Corinna angrier. "Don't you realize why we just showed you all this?" Lynda, now frustrated herself, asked Corinna, "Okay, why did I get shown all this, then?" Corinna asked, "You honestly don't know why you are here?" Lynda responded, "No." Corinna's reaction suggested she had expected Lynda to know the answer.

"You were only here to see what this is like," Corinna explained. "You have to go back and tell others about it. You're going to have a daughter who is important to us. If you stay here, she will never be born. You're not supposed to be here, in this room," Corinna continued. "You have to go."

Corinna said she was Lynda's great-great-great-great-grandmother and explained that there were important things Lynda still had to accomplish on Earth. Lynda had a purpose, and her life wasn't yet complete.

Corinna shared several glimpses of what lay ahead for Lynda, warning her of the hard tests she would face in life. Lynda felt as though the conversation lasted years, even though, in earthly time, she had been "dead" for only a few minutes. As their meeting neared its end, Corinna gestured toward something in the distance. "Don't you understand that if you go in 'there,' you can never go back?" Lynda turned to see the most mesmerizing tunnel she could imagine. She felt a deep longing to enter but realized that if she did, there would be no return.

The infinite white space around them darkened slightly, and a mist spilled gently from the tunnel's mouth. The tunnel itself appeared to be rotating both clockwise and counterclockwise. At the far end of the tunnel, a light brighter than anything she had ever seen filled her with a sense of peace and love. Lynda fought the desire to enter.

Corinna explained that entering the tunnel would set two events into motion. "If you go through this tunnel," Corinna said, "the first thing that will happen is that you will reincarnate. The second thing," Corinna continued, "is that you would sign a contract." This contract would outline the plan for Lynda's next life, detailing the lessons she would need to learn, the challenges she would face, and the experiences necessary for her growth. Every element of this plan would be carefully crafted to guide her soul's evolution. The contract symbolized not only a commitment to another earthly journey but also an agreement to face certain challenges. Lynda suddenly found herself back in the fog stage.

Only moments later, the fog faded, and Lynda opened her eyes to find herself in a hospital bed. She had awakened from an eight-day coma and returned to the physical world.

Verification Events

While Lynda's physical body lay in the ensuite bathroom, her consciousness floated near the ceiling in the living room, a location that would normally require a physical route to reach.

To physically move from the ensuite bathroom to the living room, one would have to exit the ensuite, navigate around the walk-in closet and into the main bedroom, then cross the bedroom and pass through a door leading to the living room. However, in her out-of-body state, Lynda's consciousness bypassed this route entirely, instead manifesting directly in the living room, watching events from a point near the ceiling.

The Sheriff

When the sheriff visited Lynda in the hospital, she recognized him immediately. "Hello. Nice to see you again," she greeted him.

The sheriff looked at her, puzzled, and replied, "What do you mean, see you again? This is the first time you've seen me."

Lynda responded, "No, you were in the house the other night. Thank you so much for being there."

The sheriff seemed taken aback, replying, "Well, you were in the toilet. I didn't go and see you. I was out in the living room."

Lynda asked, "What are you doing here today?"

The sheriff explained, "I actually want to see if you want to press charges because I have sufficient evidence to charge him with attempted murder."

Lynda continued, "I know that you asked him all those questions."

The sheriff, visibly shocked, asked, "How do you know I asked him all those questions?"

She replied, "Because I was in that living room, near the ceiling, watching you asking him the questions."

The sheriff asked, "Do you want to charge him with attempted murder?"

Lynda shook her head. "No, I want to go back to Australia."

The sheriff seemed further stunned by Lynda's knowledge of details he hadn't shared.

She pointed out, "You were walking like you had a limp. You kept shifting from one foot to the other like you were favoring a leg."

The sheriff asked, "Did you see that?"

Lynda simply replied, "Yes, I did see that."

This conversation left the sheriff astonished, as Lynda's observations confirmed that her consciousness had been present in the living room, noticing every detail, including those he hadn't been aware of himself.

Medical Records Confirmation

The medical records confirm Lynda had no heart rate, was not breathing, and was clinically dead for at least 14 minutes. Defibrillation, a measure taken only when the heart has stopped, was used, confirming her heart had flatlined. A brain in this condition is incapable of making and retaining complex memories, meaning traditional neuroscience would deem it impossible for Lynda to observe or remember events during this period.

Accurate Descriptions of Events

Lynda accurately recounted many details, including:

She described the sheriff's questions, conversations among the paramedics, and specific actions taken by those present, even though her body was in a separate room.

She saw the sheriff's name on his badge, noted details about the uniforms, and observed the sheriff's movements, including his limp.

As time has passed, some insights or events from Lynda's experience have reportedly come true, lending further weight to her account as a source of potentially profound knowledge about life and the future.

Reference

Lynda Cramer, (2021) *'Five Years In Heaven: The Teachings of Heaven'*

11. The Library of Lives

KAREN THOMAS

Then, she asked him if what she had seen truly happened that day. His response was immediate: "How did you know that?"

*

In 1982, Karen Thomas lived in Anchorage, Alaska, with her husband and their two children. She worked as a physical therapist in the acute physical therapy department of a hospital—a role that occasionally required her to lift patients. During one such task, she suffered a ruptured disc in her lower back. Despite undergoing therapy and receiving medication, her condition showed no signs of improvement. Having already undergone back surgery for a ruptured disc in 1977, Karen understood how serious her new injury was.

Her doctor informed her that surgery might be necessary, given her lack of progress. However, it was unclear whether a laminectomy alone would suffice or if a more extensive procedure, such as a spinal fusion, was needed. The possibility of a spinal fusion worried Karen, as it would mean a two-month recovery period and could potentially jeopardize her career.

Karen decided to proceed with the surgery and reached out to her church in New York State, as well as her family and friends, asking them to pray for her. She shared the surgery date, requesting prayers that only a laminectomy would be necessary.

On the morning of the surgery, her husband and their two young children visited her hospital room. The staff prepped her, and her family walked alongside as she was wheeled to the operating suite. The medical team carefully positioned her on her stomach for the back surgery, and a nurse inserted an IV into Karen's arm to administer the anesthetic. As the medicine took effect, Karen drifted into unconsciousness.

Suddenly, she found herself very near the ceiling in the corner of the operating room. "I was so high up I was just inches from the ceiling tiles," she recalled. From this viewpoint, she could see the medical staff rushing around her body. The doctor was swearing angrily, barking orders for the nurses to fetch more bags of blood. The medical team carefully turned Karen's body from face down to face up on the operating table.

"I realized that's me, that white face thing is me, and I'm up here, and I must be dead. I have to get to my husband and my kids. I've got to let them know that, somehow, I'm still me. I don't understand this at all, but I've got to find them. So as soon as I started thinking that, my consciousness literally went through the wall back out into the hallway I had come down."

Soon she entered another hallway, close to the waiting room where her husband and kids were waiting. A voice telepathically spoke to her and said, "Pay attention to this man." Karen watched as a man rushed out of an elevator and headed in the direction she had just come from. She zoomed in and saw every detail, his eye color, his clothing, and heard his thoughts. "He was thinking, 'I've got to get in there fast,' and as he was thinking that, I heard the thoughts of another man who was closer to the double doors, and his thoughts were, 'What's that guy think he's doing? He can't go in there, he's not a doctor, he's just dressed in regular clothes.'" The man paused at the double doors and then rushed through when they swung open.

When she attempted to go to her family in the waiting room, she found she couldn't control her direction. Instead of moving to them, a powerful force pulled her upward. She ascended through the hospital, rising through each floor until she passed through the roof and out into the open sky. As her speed increased, Karen saw the mountain range near the hospital and the city of Anchorage stretching out below her. She had the awareness of speeding through the sky, but strangely, there was no sensation of wind and she didn't feel the cold.

Karen continued to ascend until she reached a large, dark, circular hole in the sky. "Just at the point where I would have been going out over the water, a big, dark, rounded, kind of looked almost like a cave opening came in front of me, and I was sucked inside of it." She felt herself moving even faster, though once again, there was no feeling of air rushing past her. She described it as though she was moving at an incredible speed but with no physical sensations to accompany it.

Ahead, there was a pinpoint of light. Upon getting closer, the light exploded into a brilliant glow, bathing her in peace and love. "I thought, 'Well, where am I?' and looked where my feet should be. I saw a brown rocky ground below me and the whole landscape was very arid looking," Karen recalled. "My first thought was, well, this isn't what I would think heaven would be like."

A telepathic voice said, "Follow me," Karen looked up to see a man climbing a rugged hill ahead of her. He had long, dark hair pulled back with a leather tie and a toga-like garment made from coarse, off-white fabric. He wore sandals with leather straps wrapped around his calves. When she saw him, she thought, "That's not Jesus!" There was a comforting warmth in their connection, as if they were long-lost friends.

When Karen reached the top of the hill, she was greeted by a breathtaking view. The surrounding landscape was alive with vibrant green grass, dotted with colorful flowers. Tall shade trees stood nearby, offering a peaceful contrast to the bright colors of the meadow. In the distance, a river sparkled in the sunlight. As Karen approached the riverbank, she saw a large group of people gathered on the other side. Her heart lifted as she recognized her father and brother. Their faces were filled with joy when they saw her.

Looking closer, Karen noticed the group comprised many familiar faces, including her aunts, uncles, and cousins. But then, something surprising caught her attention. Among the crowd were a few people she hadn't met. These were her grandparents, all of whom had passed away before she was born. Even though she had never met them, Karen instantly recognized them. "They were all welcoming as if to say, 'Oh, wow, she's here. Isn't this wonderful? She's here.' I wanted so badly to go to them," Karen recalled. Though she couldn't remember what they were wearing or even what they looked like, their presence was unmistakable.

Karen longed to be with her loved ones, but her guide insisted they go somewhere else first. They walked together, following the curve of the river until they reached a huge open space. Close by, she caught sight of a magnificent Greek-style building supported by grand columns with many steps leading up to it. The building glowed a luminous pearlescent white. This was a hub of activity, with many spiritual beings in white robes coming and going. Her guide led her inside, where the space opened up into a vast library, its shelves filled with countless books and scrolls. Large tables covered nearly every inch of the floor space. Many spirits sat studying, each engrossed in their own book. Moving through the grand hall, her guide spoke only once to tell her that this was the location of the 'Book of Lives'.

They stepped into a smaller room, where Karen encountered a group of spiritual beings gathered around a large table. They sat in a semi-circle as though they had been patiently awaiting their arrival. Her guide turned to her and said that they were there to review her life up to this point. At the center of the table was a surface that appeared to be clear, almost like the bottom of a glass-bottomed boat. The moment her guide finished speaking, a hologram appeared displaying scenes from Karen's life. One by one, the moments she had lived unfolded. "I was able to experience myself going through all of these different events in my life and interacting with the other people I was interacting with," she explained. "Also, being able to be them or feel as though I was there. The main things I was being shown were things where either I had hurt someone by my actions or words or had helped someone. Both types of events were shown to me. I was able to really feel the pain that someone else had experienced, or the good that they carried away from our interaction, and rippled out toward all the people that they then interacted with."

As she watched the painful moments and the hurt she had caused, she saw that not a single spirit judged her for her actions. They told her that every experience, both good and bad, was a valuable part of learning and understanding others. "I got the feeling I should know this group of people," she said. "In fact, I felt as though they had helped me plan my life before I ever lived it." The spirits gave Karen a choice: she could either return to her life or stay. If she went back, they wanted to show her what might happen. Some events were certain, while others depended on the choices of those around her because everyone has free will, and individual decisions could change the path ahead.

As the visions of the future played out, she was certain she had glimpsed something important. But when she tried to remember it, the image seemed obscured, as though the spirits had deliberately blocked it. Her guide explained they would wipe her memory of the future events in her life, as the knowledge of what she had witnessed could influence her decisions. However, she was told that she would keep enough memories to satisfy her regarding the reality of her experience. In addition, they would give her an unmistakable sign, something undeniable that would serve as proof of her experience.

Suddenly, she was in a much smaller room with just her guide. "He said, before you decide whether you're going back to your life or staying here, I want to show you some things." To her right-hand side, she saw an image of all the prayers being offered by her family and friends. Each prayer sounded a musical note, all linking to form a melody.

Her guide then showed her a scene to her left. "It was as though I was looking through the ceiling of the waiting room that my husband and the kids were in," she recalled. The surgeon stood in the doorway of the waiting room in his green surgical garb, his mask removed. He spoke with her husband as their children sat nearby on a couch. Although she couldn't hear the words exchanged, their emotions were obvious.

Karen became aware of her daughter praying. She believed something had gone wrong, that the long wait for news from the doctor meant Karen hadn't survived the surgery. Her daughter's prayer formed the last link in the chain that connected all the prayers to where she was. Karen recalled that, at seven, she had prayed desperately for her father not to die.

When her father died, it felt as though her prayer had gone unanswered, leaving her to live life without him. She couldn't allow her children to experience the same fate she had, growing up without their mother, as she had grown up without her father. The realization that she couldn't leave them behind overcame her. She said, "I have to go back. I have to go back for them." With that, her next awareness was waking up in the recovery room, surrounded by her husband and children.

The intensity of her experience stayed with her for three weeks, but even after this faded, she believed her experience was real. Following her surgery, she remained in the hospital for twelve days, initially in intensive care, before moving to a regular hospital room. The situation was touch-and-go for a while, with moments of uncertainty. At first, she hesitated to share her near-death experience with her family. She recalled feeling gratitude during her first visit from the surgeon who had saved her life. They had never met before, but he was the same man she had seen rushing into the operating suite during her surgery, called in to perform the critical operation.

Verification Events

Karen's Husband

Shortly after returning home, she shared her near-death experience with her husband. She told him about the moment she had seen the surgeon arriving on the day of her surgery and asked if he remembered noticing a man rushing past the waiting room door. He recalled seeing someone move quickly by, though he hadn't been facing the doorway directly.

She recalled the scene in the waiting room where the surgeon who had operated on her had talked to her husband while their children sat on a couch. She said the surgeon was in his green surgical garb, and his mask was missing. Though she couldn't hear the conversation, she could clearly see the emotion on their faces. Karen asked him if the doctor had worn green surgical garb, including a hairnet-style hat, but without a mask. He confirmed that, yes, the doctor had been dressed just like that. Her husband told her the surgeon had asked for his permission to proceed with the additional surgery needed to save her life.

The Surgeon

About a week after she returned home, she visited the surgeon's office to have the staples removed from her incision. After he completed the examination, she shared her unusual experience with him, explaining that during the resuscitation, she felt her spirit had left her body and traveled outside the operating room.

She described to him how she had seen him arrive that day, recalling in detail how he had hurried toward the operating room suite dressed in street clothes, a brown jacket, and carrying a bag. She mentioned noticing his expression, noting how he seemed frustrated to be slowed down near the doors to the operating room. The surgeon said he had rushed down the stairs and had to slow down to press the button to open the automatic doors leading to the operating suite.

Karen asked about the other man there, but he didn't recall another man being near the entry to the operating room. She thought it was likely they did not speak to each other at all and realized she was probably 'hearing' both of their thoughts simultaneously through telepathy, which led her to believe they were conversing. She was picking up on the surgeon's thoughts about needing to get into the operating room quickly, as well as the other man's concerns about a person in street clothes not having the right to enter.

Then, she asked him if what she had seen truly happened that day. His response was immediate: "How did you know that?" He explained that he had been at his office when he received a page to come to the operating room urgently. Emergency surgery was required to find and stop the bleeding from an artery that had been cut during the procedure. What stood out to her was that he never explicitly confirmed whether he was wearing the brown jacket she had described.

Instead, he simply repeated, "How did you know that?" Her story clearly left him astonished, and she was sure if he hadn't been wearing the brown jacket or if events hadn't unfolded just as she described, he would have been quick to correct her.

Her Gynecologist

During her follow-up visit with her gynecologist, he asked about the recent abdominal scar from her surgery. When she explained what had happened, he said, "That was YOU! I was in the adjacent operating room that day and heard all hell breaking loose in there. The air was blue for a while, I can tell you!" Although she didn't share her near-death experience with him during that visit, his reaction verified what she had seen in the operating room, including the swearing.

12. The Multicolored Tunnel and the Angel Named Elizabeth

KRISTLE MERZLOCK

She described the details with such clarity: the clothes they were wearing, the exact positions they were in around the house, and even the meal her mother was preparing. Her parents were astonished that she could so clearly recall these details, even though she had been unconscious in the hospital.

*

On March 13, 1982, seven-year-old Kristle Merzlock was at a birthday party at the YMCA swimming pool in Pocatello, Idaho. She was excited to test the swimming skills she had learned in her lessons at school and ventured toward the deep end of the pool. As she neared the edge, a group of boys playing nearby accidentally bumped into her, causing her to lose her balance and fall into the water. Kristle panicked and tried to swim to the surface, but her movements only made things worse. In her struggle to breathe, she swallowed water and soon lost consciousness.

The adults at the party quickly noticed Kristle floating face down in the water and pulled her out of the pool. Fortunately, a doctor was present, who immediately began administering CPR and gave her sodium bicarbonate to stabilize her. An ambulance transported Kristle to one of the Seattle Children's Hospital clinics, where Dr. Melvin Morse, a critical care physician and pediatrician known for his expertise in resuscitation, was called in to manage her care.

Dr. Morse and his team worked quickly to try and resuscitate Kristle, but with each passing minute, her chances of survival were decreasing. Her vital signs were fading, and her pupils were fixed and dilated, showing no sign of brain activity. Dr. Morse used a defibrillator to shock her heart back to life, and he connected Kristle to an artificial lung machine to help her breathe. They quickly performed a CAT scan, which revealed severe swelling in her brain and little to no cerebral activity. After a short time on the artificial lung, she developed adult respiratory distress syndrome. This caused her lungs to swell, and with prolonged periods of low oxygen, her blood became acidified, putting her in an even more dangerous state. For over four hours, Kristle's body struggled against the severe damage caused by the lack of oxygen.

Kristle remained unresponsive, showing little reaction to any stimuli. When she was in pain, her body contorted into abnormal positions, showing a low level of consciousness. Dr. Morse assessed her condition using the Glasgow Coma Scale, giving her a score of 5, which suggested she had very limited awareness. Based on her critical state, Dr. Morse knew her chances of survival were slim. Even if she survived, the prolonged lack of oxygen and severe brain swelling likely meant she would suffer permanent brain damage.

Dr. Morse consulted with specialists at Seattle Children's Hospital by telephone. After discussing her case, he proceeded with an arterial catheterization to monitor her condition more closely. Once Kristle stabilized, the medical team moved her to the Primary Children's Hospital in Salt Lake City, where she could receive more specialized care for her critical injuries.

The NDE

Kristle found herself surrounded by complete darkness. Eerie, indescribable sounds echoed all around her, filling her with fear. But just as panic set in, everything shifted. Suddenly, she was in a tunnel made of transparent bricks. Bright, multicolored lights shone from the outside, casting a glowing light through the walls of the tunnel. Ahead of her, she saw a brilliant light that seemed to radiate love and warmth. The floor of the tunnel was uneven, making it difficult for Kristle to walk. She crawled along, inching her way toward the light. After a few feet, she saw a figure appear ahead, a tall woman with blonde hair who reached out, took Kristle's hand, and helped her to her feet.

The woman introduced herself as Elizabeth and explained that she was Kristle's guardian angel, sent to help guide her. Elizabeth led Kristle forward, and as they reached the light, Kristle saw an astonishing scene unfold before her. Green meadows stretched out in all directions, filled with vibrant flowers. A waterfall flowed peacefully in the distance, and trees heavy with white fruit stood around the landscape.

People dressed in white robes moved through the scene, radiating warmth and a sense of welcome. Kristle felt an overwhelming sense of love and belonging, as if she had returned home, and everything around her felt oddly familiar.

There was a boundary surrounding her location. She could see beyond the boundary, but she instinctively understood that crossing it was not possible. Family members gathered to greet her, including aunts and uncles, as well as a grandmother she had never met. Her recently departed Aunt Pat was there, along with her grandfather, Paul, and one of her uncle's friends, named George. They were all excited and joyful to see her. Throughout this, Elizabeth, her guardian angel, remained by her side.

As Kristle continued to explore, two girls around her age approached her. They introduced themselves as Heather and Melissa and said they would soon be born on Earth. Kristle immediately felt a strong connection with them and thought of them as her playmates in heaven. Heather and Melissa introduced her to many other people.

During her experience, she found herself with Jesus, who held her on his lap. He asked her if she wished to stay. Kristle immediately answered, "Yes, why would I ever want to leave?" But then, thoughts of her mother came flooding back, and Kristle realized she needed to return to be with her. Jesus and the Heavenly Father explained that if she went back, she should honor her parents and strive to be a good person. Though she wanted to stay, she understood her journey on

Earth wasn't complete, and she accepted she should return. Kristle described the Heavenly Father as an elderly man with long white hair and a flowing beard.

As Kristle began her return, she found herself able to look down on Dr. Morse and observe the treatment he was administering in the hospital. She watched as they intubated her, and she realized, "I wasn't dead, I wasn't dead at all. Some part of me was still alive."

Kristle travelled to her home during her experience. She saw her brothers and sisters playing in their rooms. One of her brothers was moving a GI Joe around in a jeep. In another room, one of her sisters was combing the hair of her Barbie doll while singing along to a rock song. Kristle then drifted into the kitchen, where she saw her mother preparing a meal of roast chicken and rice. Next, she looked into the living room and saw her father sitting on the couch, staring quietly ahead. She couldn't help but feel that he was deeply worried about her, waiting for news from the hospital.

The sequence of Kristle's experiences was hard for her to place in order.

Three days after being admitted to Primary Children's Hospital in Salt Lake City, Kristle awoke from her coma. The nurses in the intensive care unit said that her first words upon awakening were, "Where are Heather and Melissa?" Throughout her hospital stay, Kristle continually asked about Heather and Melissa, and at one point, the nurses called her mother into the room, responding to Kristle's calls for her.

However, upon her mother's arrival, Kristle was actually calling for Heather, not her mother.

Just two days after waking from her coma, Kristle had made remarkable progress and showed no signs of permanent brain damage. She made an amazing recovery, considering that only a small number out of every 300 patients in the same situation fully recovered. Doctors discharged Kristle from the hospital only seven days later. Upon returning home, the hospital assigned specialists to visit her to assess her condition. However, after completing their evaluations, they questioned why they had been called in the first place, as they found Kristle to be in excellent health.

Verification Events

Meeting Dr. Morse

Two weeks after returning home, Kristle went to the Pocatello clinic for a follow-up examination. Although Dr. Morse wasn't scheduled to meet her that day, he was delighted to see her in the hallway. He was genuinely surprised to see her looking like a normal young girl, with no apparent signs of what had happened to her. Approaching her, he introduced himself, mentioning that she might not remember him, but he certainly remembered her. Kristle turned to her mother and said, "That's the one with the beard, Mom! First, there was this tall doctor who didn't have a beard, and then he came in. He was putting things in my wrist and down my mouth." Her recollection was accurate. Dr. Morse did indeed have a beard, while the doctor who initially attended to her did not. When Dr. Morse asked her if she remembered what had happened at the swimming pool, she responded, "You mean when I visited the Heavenly Father?"

Despite her eyes being closed and having been profoundly comatose during the entire ordeal, Kristle confidently stated that she had "seen" everything that was happening around her. She described her experience in detail, recounting how they moved her from a large room to a smaller one and then took X-rays. She shared that she had listened to the phone call during which Dr. Morse consulted with Seattle Children's Hospital and accurately recounted the conversations he had with both doctors and nurses in the clinic. Kristle also remembered her nasal intubation, noting that Dr. Morse had used this method, which was less common; about 90% of other doctors typically employed throat intubation.

Visit Home

During her near-death experience, Kristle visited her home, where she roamed through the house and watched her brothers and sisters playing with their toys in their rooms. One of her brothers was playing with a GI Joe, pushing the action figure around the room in a jeep, while one of her sisters combed the hair of her Barbie doll, singing along to a popular rock song. As she drifted to the kitchen, Kristle saw her mother preparing a meal of roast chicken and rice. Then she looked in the living room and saw her father sitting on the couch, staring quietly ahead. Kristle sensed he was worrying about her while she was in the hospital.

Later, when Kristle shared her experience with her parents, they were stunned. She described the details with such clarity: the clothes they were wearing, the exact positions they were in around the house, and even the meal her mother was preparing. Her parents were astonished that she could so clearly recall these details, even though she had been unconscious in the hospital.

Reference

AJ Parr, (2024) *The Girl Who Visited Heaven And Other Children's Near-Death Experiences'*

13. From the Spider's Sting to the Ocean of Souls

RYAN MCCULLY

The room fell silent, his girlfriend's expression shifting from confusion to astonishment. She knew he hadn't physically been there during that conversation, yet here he was, recounting it word for word.

*

Ryan McCully had spent a relaxed evening at a friend's house. The next morning, he noticed two unusual marks on his skin, resembling bite marks. While they were uncomfortable, he thought little of them and went on with his day. The following morning, the marks hadn't faded or shown any signs of improvement, but Ryan continued to ignore them. On the third day, however, everything changed. Ryan experienced sharp, intense stomach pains that quickly worsened. Concerned by the sudden severity of his symptoms, he went to the hospital. After evaluating both his pain and the strange bite marks, the doctors informed him that his condition was far more serious than he had initially realized.

After a thorough examination, the medical team grew concerned that Ryan's deteriorating condition might be because of a poisonous spider bite. They quickly ran tests, and the results confirmed their fears. Ryan had developed two dangerous abscesses, which posed a serious risk to his health. The doctors decided he needed surgery immediately to remove the infected tissue and prevent further complications. As the medical staff prepped Ryan for surgery, he lay on the gurney, looking at the ceiling lights above him. The anesthesia took effect, softening the bright lights and dulling the surrounding sounds. Slowly, he slipped into unconsciousness.

Awareness returned and Ryan found himself in a vast, spiritual space. He saw an endless, shimmering ocean of souls stretching out in every direction. These souls moved elegantly, swirling and shifting within a vast energy field that seemed to pulse with life. It was an energy beyond understanding, full of purpose. Each soul seemed guided by an unseen force as it moved through the realm. Some were heading to Earth to begin new journeys, while others were returning from their last life, crossing back over the veil.

Even within the boundless expanse of souls, Ryan found he could distinctly perceive each individual. He focused on one soul, and in an instant, her face came into view as if she were mere inches from him. She appeared to be a woman in her late fifties, and as she noticed Ryan's attention, she turned to face him. A kindness filled her gaze. She smiled softly and gave a slight nod, a gesture that seemed to convey an understanding. Ryan felt an instinctive connection and returned her greeting with his own smile and nod, as if they were old friends.

As Ryan took in his surroundings, he realized distinct levels as if it were a crossing point between realms. In one area, he noticed souls moving with purposeful energy, a place filled with activity and focus, where individuals seemed to prepare for new journeys or reflect on those already lived. Souls came and went, and the space felt charged with life. Another realm radiated an intense, all-encompassing light that seemed full of peace. This light washed over everything, creating a deep calm, and Ryan felt himself drawn to this place. The peace extended through him, beyond the edges of this space, reaching every corner of the universe. It was as if he were with an eternal presence, knowing that everything was exactly as it should be.

There was an intense longing to remain. However, while he struggled with the yearning to stay, a strong feeling emerged in him. It was as if he were receiving a subtle, unspoken message, not an outright command, but an understanding that while staying was an option, it wasn't truly where he was meant to be. Deep down, he sensed that the right decision was to go back. A vision of his family came to him. At that moment, Ryan realized that returning wasn't just about his journey but also about the lives of his family and friends.

Curious about his family gathered in the hospital, Ryan found himself transported there effortlessly, as if his thoughts had guided him. In this out-of-body state, he drifted into the waiting room and saw his loved ones. He noticed his girlfriend talking with his aunt, frustration clear in her voice as she explained how her mother often used scripture to make her feel guilty, using it as a form of manipulation. His aunt listened and offered advice and support. As Ryan watched, he nodded in agreement with his aunt, even commenting aloud on what she was saying.

With a sense of reluctance, Ryan drifted toward his body and felt himself slowly merge back into it. As soon as he regained consciousness, he abruptly sat up, catching the nurses off guard. They hadn't expected him to wake for some time. In those first moments, he felt oddly detached from his body. Simple movements were hard, and he struggled to coordinate his limbs, likening the sensation to trying to move with chopsticks, clumsy and imprecise.

The lights in the room felt intensely bright, so much so that he closed his eyes. But, to his amazement, he found he could still "see" the surrounding room, as well as glimpses of other parts of the hospital, feeling his awareness extended beyond his body. It was as if he were only partly anchored to his physical form, still keeping some of the heightened perception he'd experienced in the spiritual realm. When he was transferred to the recovery room, his odd awareness gradually faded, and he connected fully to his body.

As Ryan's family gathered around his bed, checking on his condition, he suddenly noticed a presence beside him: his deceased grandmother. She appeared with a gentle aura, and her first words to him were a request to pass along a message to his aunt. "Tell her not to be so sad," she said. "Let her know it's not my wish for her to spend all night in tears." When Ryan shared this message with his aunt, her reaction was one of astonishment. She revealed that, despite putting on a brave face, she had been deeply grieving losing her mother, spending many sleepless nights crying, a secret she hadn't shared with anyone.

Shortly after, another familiar presence appeared, this time his grandmother on his mother's side. Yet she looked different, not as he remembered her, but as a beautiful young woman. Her youthful appearance struck Ryan. He had never seen a picture of her from that time. She didn't bring a message, only a gentle smile, showing him a version of herself that still thrived in the spiritual realm. One by one, other deceased family members visited, each bringing messages of reassurance, guidance, or love for those they had left behind.

The effort of moving his body was exhausting. Now and then, he would step out of his body to rest, hovering nearby to regain his strength. From this vantage point, he watched his physical form, continuing to talk with the family members gathered around his hospital bed. His body would nod, smile, and respond to their words, engaged in the conversation as though nothing unusual was happening. It was an unsettling experience, watching himself communicate with no direction from his spirit. Despite having no influence over his body's actions, he felt a part of everything it said and did, as if somehow he remained connected.

Verification Events

His Girlfriend and Aunt

In the weeks following his return home, Ryan found that the memories of his near-death experience were hazy, like fragments of a half-remembered dream. It wasn't until one afternoon, as he was talking with his girlfriend, that an important piece of it resurfaced. She was venting about how her mother had been trying to manipulate her by quoting scripture and using guilt to control her. As she spoke, a vague memory came to Ryan. He interrupted, saying, "We don't have to go over this again. I was there when my aunt gave you advice." His girlfriend looked at him, puzzled, as he repeated his aunt's exact words, "She told you to study the Bible yourself so you could quote parts back to your mother."

The room fell silent, his girlfriend's expression shifting from confusion to astonishment. She knew he hadn't physically been there during that conversation, yet here he was, recounting it word for word. At that moment, Ryan felt the clarity of the memory flooding back. She stared at him, clearly bewildered. "You couldn't have known that," she said. But Ryan was certain. He insisted he had been there and even recalled commenting to himself that his aunt was giving brilliant advice. He described the waiting room in vivid detail, the exact arrangement of the chairs, the position of the TV, and how only half of the lights were on. He even mentioned that the lights were dim because his aunt had complained about the brightness.

As he recounted these details, his girlfriend's face paled. She told him that the conversation had taken place in the hospital while he was in surgery, unconscious. The lights had been dimmed specifically because his aunt had found them too bright, a detail he couldn't possibly have known from his hospital bed. Ryan realized he had genuinely been out of his body and witnessed events as they unfolded in the physical world. There was no other explanation. He had seen and heard things he couldn't possibly have known otherwise.

Grandmother

He passed on a message from his deceased grandmother to his aunt. "Tell her not to be so sad. Let her know it's not my wish for her to spend all night in tears." Ryan's aunt was astonished. She revealed that, despite putting on a brave face, she had been deeply grieving her mother's death, spending many sleepless nights crying, a secret she hadn't shared with anyone.

*

Over the three months of his recovery, Ryan often reflected on his near-death experience, sensing that every element had been purposeful. He came to believe that what he had seen, heard, and felt was exactly what he was meant to receive, no more, no less. Yet he couldn't shake the feeling that some memories remain hidden, guarded by the spirit world for reasons he might never fully understand. Ryan wondered if he remembered only what he should remember, as if the spiritual realm had revealed only certain truths while withholding others until he was ready or perhaps never revealing them at all.

14. The Garden of What Is and What Could Be

AMBER CAVANAGH

"Every single person has confirmed that what I saw actually was happening at the time."

*

In 2021, Amber Cavanagh lived in Nanaimo, Canada, with her husband, Mike, and their two children. On December 23, while watching a Christmas movie with her kids, she developed a very intense headache. Later, she found out it was caused by a tear in her carotid artery. As the pain grew worse, Amber went to bed, hoping the rest would bring some relief. An hour later, she texted Mike, asking him to bring home Tylenol and Advil, but shortly after sending the message, she lost consciousness.

Doctors later estimated that Amber's stroke had occurred around 11:30 p.m. But it wasn't until 4:45 a.m. that she woke up, feeling a strange sensation spreading through her body. When she tried to move, she realized her right arm and leg weren't responding. At first, she thought it might just be sleep paralysis.

Hoping to snap herself out of it, Amber got up to go to the bathroom. "I thought, Okay, I need to get to the bathroom because maybe it'll wake me up," she later recalled. But as soon as she tried to stand, she collapsed to the floor, her body completely paralyzed on one side. Mike, her husband, had fallen asleep on the couch in the room next to their bedroom. Amber tried to drag herself to the door, but it was a struggle, and she couldn't get far. Using her left arm, she started banging on the wall, hoping to make enough noise for him to hear. Mike woke up and rushed in to find Amber on the floor. She tried to explain what was happening but could only say her sister's name, "Michelle." Mike, a trained level three first aid attendant, performed basic stroke tests to check Amber's responses, but she couldn't react to any of them. He immediately called 911 for help.

The ambulance took longer than expected to arrive, and Mike called 911 again. Amber could see his frustration building, his concern turning to anger with each passing minute. When the paramedics finally arrived, their response was dismissive. Despite Mike's insistence that Amber had suffered a stroke, they seemed unconcerned and didn't take the situation seriously. "My husband kept saying, 'Yes, it is!'" Amber recalled. "Mike told them, 'Have her raise her arms. She can only raise one. Smile? Talk? She can't do any of that.'" But the paramedics didn't seem to take him seriously. They assumed Amber was drunk or high on pills. "Because we live in a nice area, they thought I was just a drunk housewife at Christmas," she said. Despite Mike's repeated insistence that something was seriously wrong, the paramedics were unfazed. They moved slowly and handled Amber with little urgency as they got her into the ambulance.

During the ambulance ride, the paramedics continued to downplay the seriousness of Amber's condition. They moved at a slow pace, with no lights or sirens, as if it were a routine transport. To make matters worse, they failed to notify the hospital that Amber might be having a stroke. Desperate, Amber held the medic's hand and locked eyes with him. "He looked into my eyes," Amber recalled. "All of a sudden, he looks scared. He said, 'I think it actually might be a stroke.'" However, the driver replied, "Oh, no, it's not. She's just drunk."

When the ambulance finally reached the hospital, the paramedics parked Amber's trolley in triage amongst many others and began chatting casually with the medical staff. It wasn't until a nurse glanced over and noticed the severe drooping on Amber's face that the seriousness of her situation became clear. "A nurse turned around and looked at the EMTs and said, 'What the fuck are you guys doing? She's obviously having a stroke,'" Amber recalled. "By then, my face had started really drooping." The nurse immediately called a stroke code, and the medical team rushed Amber for a brain scan, which confirmed the extent of her condition. She had suffered a massive stroke on the left side of her brain, with a secondary stroke affecting her frontal lobe. The medical team began emergency protocols right away, working against the clock to stabilize her and minimize the damage.

In stroke cases, timing is everything. If treated within the first three to four hours, a medication called TPA (Tissue Plasminogen Activator) can dissolve the clot and sometimes reverse the effects of the stroke. Unfortunately for Amber, her stroke happened around 11:30 p.m., but she didn't arrive at the hospital until 5:30 a.m., well past the window for TPA treatment. This delay meant that the chance to prevent lasting damage was gone.

When Mike and Amber's sister, Michelle, arrived at the hospital, the doctor explained the option of administering TPA, at this moment the doctors weren't totally sure what time the Stroke happened, they guessed it could have been within the last two hours. He warned them of the significant risks, including potential side effects that could be fatal. Knowing how serious Amber's condition was, Mike agreed that TPA was their best hope to stop the progression of her stroke. They gave the medication, hoping it had only been a couple of hours since it had started.

It successfully stopped the secondary stroke from getting worse, but it was too late for the first one. The medical staff told Mike that Amber urgently needed brain surgery, but their hospital didn't have the facilities for such a complex procedure. The only option was to airlift her to a specialized hospital. Mike didn't hesitate and immediately agreed.

When the helicopter arrived, Mike stayed close to Amber as they moved her across the tarmac. He climbed into the cabin and took a seat next to her. As they lifted off, the morning sun poured through the windows, filling the cabin with bright light. Mike noticed the sun shining on Amber's face and raised his hand to shield her eyes.

In that moment, Amber found herself in a stunning, otherworldly garden. "I didn't have to go to the light," she explained. "One moment, I was in my body, and the next, I was gone. I just opened my eyes and was on the other side." The garden was alive with colors more vivid than anything she had ever seen. "The closest thing I can compare it to is maybe 'Avatar' at nighttime," she said. "Everything glowed, the trees, the grass, they radiated this golden rainbow light that felt like the light of God."

Amber felt intensely connected to everything around her. Every tree, stone, and blade of grass seemed alive, each humming with its own energy. Looking down at herself, she noticed she was in a much younger body, which she described as the angelic version of herself. She was wearing a white, off-the-shoulder dress, her bare feet rested on the soft grass. Without warning a stream of knowledge, greater than anything Amber had ever known, flooded her mind. She saw the impact of every thought, word, and action she had ever taken. Even her smallest choices had shaped her life in significant ways, with each one leading to a different outcome. She could see how her decisions had created ripples that spread outward, touching the lives of those around her.

In the distance, Amber saw her family, their pet dog, and her friends. She knew right away that they weren't dead.

Instead, she felt she was seeing their higher selves, their spiritual forms. They stood there quietly, not moving closer or trying to talk to her. "It wasn't like they're just standing there like a human was going, 'Oh, I wonder what's going on for her.' They were actively taking part in what I was going through without words or, you know, human niceties." Amber felt confident that her connection to them would remain, even if she stayed here or returned to her life on Earth.

In another part of the garden, Amber noticed a group she didn't recognize. They wore clothing from different time periods. Some didn't look human but appeared to be beings from other planets or dimensions. At first, Amber felt confused about who they were or why they were there. But even though she didn't recognize them, she had a strong feeling of familiarity. As Amber watched the group, a powerful realization came to her: she could feel a part of her own soul within each of them. She understood these figures were her past and future lives, each carrying a piece of her essence. They were all connected to her, their journeys linked across time and space. "Even though they're just standing there, they are feeling everything I'm feeling," Amber explained. "They're feeling my decision-making. They're feeling everything because, in this place, you can feel everything from everyone."

Amber suddenly moved to another location and found herself standing beside a beautiful gazebo, her spirit guides close by. A small stream gently flowed beneath from a nearby pond, its crystal-clear blue water sparkling in the light. She sat on the bench inside the gazebo, her guides seated either side of her. She looked out at her family and ancestors, feeling a deep sense of peace and connection. The guides didn't speak but communicated with her telepathically. They explained that her physical state was barely holding on and that she had come to this place to find rest from the trauma her body was going through.

Amber's spirit guides presented her with a choice: to return to Earth or stay in this peaceful, loving place. With her expanded understanding, she realized that time and space didn't really matter in this realm. Whether she stayed or returned, the bond with her loved ones would remain. Her guides then gave her a glimpse of the future. They showed her what her husband's life would be like if she didn't return and how her children's lives might be without her. The guides also showed her what her life would be like if she returned to Earth. They warned her that the first 18 months would be incredibly challenging. It wouldn't be easy, they said, but they also reassured her she had the strength to face whatever occurred. Her guides also explained that if she went back, her life would carry great meaning. She would have many opportunities to help others and make a positive difference in their lives.

She understood it would be okay if she stayed and that whatever choice she made would be accepted with love and understanding. There was no judgment, and there was no 'wrong' choice. "As soon as you're there, there are no questions," Amber explained. "The word 'why' disappears because you understand everything, not just about this life, but about every other life as well." She asked herself, "What does my soul need right now? Is it important for me to go back?" She thought about her purpose and the lessons she still had to share with others. Amber decided to return to her life. The moment she made that decision, she found herself in a waiting room filled with brilliant white light.

*

The helicopter landed at the hospital in Victoria, and Amber watched from above as her body was moved inside. A medical team was waiting nearby, ready to take action. Mike followed closely as she was transferred into a bed in the ICU. Within minutes, Amber's body went into a grand mal seizure. "I could see myself lying there," she said. "Then the seizure started. I watched it. As soon as it was done, I was back in my body. But before that, after making my choice, I had gone from the garden to the light-filled waiting area, and then I was up near the ceiling, watching everything. I was very close to my body, but I wasn't in it." Moments after the seizure ended, her body fell still, and she remained unconscious. Her guides later told her that if she had chosen not to return to life, the brain damage from the repeated seizures would have been fatal.

Amber's recovery was incredible. Even though her brain was badly damaged, she regained important abilities. The stroke destroyed the middle part of the left side of her brain and part of her frontal lobe. The left middle cerebral artery in her brain had completely blocked, causing a large stroke. This left an orange-sized space in one part of her brain and a smaller, thumb-sized gap in the front.

Despite all the damage, Amber can still talk, walk, and eat. Her recovery shocked everyone, including her doctors, who didn't think she would regain so much after such a severe stroke. In the 18 months after leaving the hospital, she experienced several mini-strokes, which often sent her back to the emergency room. "They have no idea how I can talk or walk or eat or anything," Amber said. "I do have a lot of deficits, so it's not all perfect. But I shouldn't be able to do any of the things that I can do." Her neurologist, with over 25 years of experience, admitted he had never seen a case like hers. Amber's recovery went beyond what medical science could explain.

Verification Events

Connect To Family

While Amber was being airlifted to the surgical hospital, her family and friends drove the two-hour trip by car. Along the way, they had to pass through the Malahat mountains, where there was no cell service. This left her sisters unable to contact Mike or find out if Amber was still alive. During this time, Amber had an extraordinary experience. She could see and hear her family from a distance, even though they were in the car. She could sense their thoughts with incredible clarity, almost as if she were right there with them.

"I could see them bargaining," Amber said. "That's what people do in stressful situations. Even if they're not religious, they start bargaining with God, saying, 'If you let her live, I'll do this, this, and that.' They weren't saying it out loud, especially with others in the car, but I could hear it in their minds. I felt their stress, their sadness, all of it as if it were my own." After she was released from the hospital, Amber shared what she had seen and felt with her family. They confirmed that what she described had actually happened, leaving them amazed by her experience.

Seizure

Amber's helicopter landed at the hospital, and she was taken to a room with Mike staying by her side. Not long after, she suffered a grand mal seizure. From a place above the room, surrounded by light, Amber observed everything that had happened. A few days later, she told Mike what she had seen. "Seizures look really painful," she said. Even though she had never regained consciousness in that room, Amber described the room in detail, including how Mike had reacted and where he and the nurse were standing. Mike confirmed that everything she described was accurate.

Children Packing

While Amber was being transported in the helicopter, her two children, aged 12 and 14, went home from the hospital to pack clothes for her. Later, Amber described what she had seen during this time. "I could see my daughter struggling to decide what to pack, unsure of what I would need," she said. She also saw her daughter speaking gently to her younger brother, trying to reassure him, even though she was clearly feeling stressed herself. The suitcase her children packed was never brought to the surgical hospital, so Amber couldn't have known what happened unless she had somehow seen it herself. Yet, she described the scene in vivid detail, as if she had been right there in the room with them. She recounted their actions and emotions while she was critically ill and being transported by helicopter. When she later shared what she had witnessed, her children confirmed everything she said.

The Family Dog

On December 29th, Mike visited Amber in the hospital, clearly upset. When he entered the room, he told her the sad news that their beloved pet dog had passed away. To his surprise, Amber started laughing softly. "That specific dog was with me on the other side," she explained. "I couldn't understand why she was there with all my other dogs who had passed." Amber had already seen their dog in the spirit realm, peacefully surrounded by her other pets, who had passed away before. She reassured Mike, saying, "Oh, that's totally fine. I saw her there, so obviously, she was ready, and now she's good."

*

For months after her stroke, Amber kept revisiting her out-of-body experiences, often asking her family to recount specific events. "I wanted them to talk me through it so I could piece everything together," she said. "I knew I wasn't physically there when you were packing, and I wasn't in the car with you. I needed either confirmation or for someone to say, 'No, that didn't actually happen.' I made them go over it until they felt crazy." Surprisingly, every family member confirmed that everything Amber described had truly happened while she was out of her body. Their confirmations grounded Amber's experiences, reinforcing her belief that she had actually witnessed these events, even though she wasn't physically present for any of them.

Amber shared her unique perspective on what she experienced, particularly her understanding of time and space. "People often understand that there's no sense of time on the other side," she explained. "But the concept of space is much harder to grasp. There was no separation of space. I could see and be everywhere, all at once. That's really difficult for people to understand while we're here."

For Amber, space didn't work the way it does here on Earth. She could see things happening in different places at the same time, as if distance didn't exist. Everything felt connected, and she could witness her family's actions, her dog's passing, and even her own physical body in the hospital all at once. It was as if she was everywhere, with no barriers or limits.

Reference

VERIFIED NEAR DEATH EXPERIENCES

Amber Cavanagh, (2023) *'At the Stroke of Eternity: One Woman's Remarkable Near-Death Experience and the Divine Messages Received'*.

15. Standstill Between Two Worlds

PAMELA REYNOLDS

This observation left the medical team astonished. Pam's ability to recount such specific details of the conversation, despite the physical barriers, was something they could not explain through any ordinary sensory perception.

*

In 1991, Pam Reynolds, a singer/songwriter from Atlanta, Georgia, had been suffering from symptoms that puzzled her doctors. After trying many treatments, the debilitating headaches, dizziness, and exhaustion persisted. A CAT scan revealed a giant basilar artery aneurysm lodged at the base of her skull. The basilar artery is part of the blood supply system for the brain and central nervous system, formed where the two vertebral arteries join at the bottom of the skull. Pam's doctor informed her that her life expectancy was very limited. He advised her to prepare herself and spend quality time with her children.

Determined to overcome this diagnosis, Pam searched for a neurosurgeon willing to help her. She soon found Dr. Robert F. Spetzler at the Barrow Neurological Institute in Phoenix, Arizona, who was considered one of the world's leading neurosurgeons. Having an aneurysm at the basilar artery is a grave condition, and Dr. Spetzler immediately recognized that standard surgical procedures would not be possible in her case. He proposed a procedure known as deep hypothermic cardiac arrest, a technique he had developed and referred to as 'Standstill'. This innovative approach involved cooling the body to a temperature that would effectively slow down her metabolism and allow for a period of cardiac arrest during which surgery could be safely performed.

To reduce metabolic demand, they would stop her heart, cool her body to about 60 degrees Fahrenheit, and drain all the blood from her head. In this state, her brain activity would completely cease, confirmed by EEG (electroencephalogram) readings, rendering her clinically dead. This extreme measure would create a 'standstill' condition that allowed Dr. Spetzler the time and stability needed to operate on the aneurysm without the risk of rupture or damage to surrounding tissues. After repairing the aneurysm, the team would then carefully reverse the procedure, rewarming Pam's body, restarting her heartbeat, and reviving her, essentially bringing her back to life.

To perform the high-risk surgery, Dr. Spetzler gathered a large team of over twenty medical professionals. This team included doctors, nurses, and technical staff, all of whom had a critical role in the procedure. The surgery required perfect coordination, as it would involve carefully monitoring Pam's vital signs, regulating her body temperature, draining and reintroducing blood, and closely tracking her brain activity. Dr. Spetzler's team was one of the most experienced in the field, and they were fully prepared to assist him in carrying out this life-saving operation.

As Pam's surgery began, the medical team carefully prepared her for the complex procedure ahead. First, they taped her eyes shut to protect them during the operation. Then, the medical team placed Pam under deep anesthesia. Next, the team began the critical step of lowering her body temperature. To manage this process, the team connected Pam to a heart-lung machine. The machine circulated her blood, cooling it as it passed through to lower her body temperature even further. This step was essential to reduce the risk of brain damage.

To carefully monitor Pam's brain activity during surgery, the medical team used a technique called auditory evoked potentials. This involved playing a loud, continuous clicking sound directly into her ears through specially molded earbuds. The sound was so loud that, under normal circumstances, it would drown out any conversation in the room. It acted as a constant stimulus, allowing the doctors to track responses from Pam's brain and to be sure there was no unintended brain activity.

As the procedure progressed to its critical stage, Dr. Spetzler stopped Pam's heart and drained the blood from her brain. This brought Pam into a state of complete clinical death, confirmed by her EEG readings, which flatlined. Her brain activity ceased entirely, and her heart was still. Pam was no longer alive in any conventional sense.

It was during her time at Standstill that she had a remarkable Near-Death Experience.

"The next thing I recall was the sound. It was a natural 'D,'" Pam remembered. "As I listened to the sound, I felt it pulling me out of the top of my head. The further out of my body I got, the clearer the tone became. I had the impression it was like a road, a frequency that you go on."

Pam described a distinct sensation when leaving her body as if there was a sudden "pop." She hovered above the operating table, looking down on herself as the surgery continued. The clarity of her perception astonished her. She could see the doctors and nurses moving around her body, and despite the state of clinical death, she experienced an awareness sharper than anything she'd known.

"I remember seeing several things in the operating room when I was looking down. It was the most aware that I think I have ever been in my entire life," Pam recalled. "I was metaphorically sitting on the doctor's shoulder. It wasn't like normal vision. It was brighter, more focused, and clearer than normal vision. There was so much in the operating room that I didn't recognize and so many people."

The room's details were incredibly vivid. She took in the unfamiliar equipment and the movements of the surgical team. Pam described seeing surgical instruments arranged on a tray. She could even make out the unique shape and structure of the bone saw. "I thought the way they had my head shaved was very peculiar," she recalled. "I expected them to take all the hair, but they did not."

She watched as the doctor cut into her skull with the strangely shaped saw, which she compared to an electric toothbrush. "The saw-thing that I hated the sound of looked like an electric toothbrush, and it had a dent in it, a groove at the top where the saw appeared to go into the handle, but it didn't," Pam said. "The saw had interchangeable blades, too, but these blades were in what looked like a socket wrench case. I heard the saw crank up. I didn't see them use it on my head, but I think I heard it being used on something. It was humming at a relatively high pitch, and then all of a sudden, it went 'Brrrrrrrrr!' like that."

The surgical team needed a specific amount of blood flow for the heart-lung machine, and they had planned to access it through an artery in Pam's leg. Recalling the moment, Pam described hearing a female voice say, "Her arteries and veins are too small," to which Dr. Spetzler responded, "Use the other side."

Pam watched the surgical activity around her leg rather than her head, where she expected the operation to be. "At that time, I was afraid because it was a brain surgery, and I saw them operate on the leg," she explained. "I was afraid that they had made a mistake and were operating in the wrong place. There were too many people, so I couldn't see what he was doing on the leg. I just knew they weren't operating in the right place, and to tell you the truth, it was terrifying. Just after hearing that my veins and my arteries were too small, I saw a tiny dot of light, and I heard a voice calling me. But I didn't hear her call me with my ears. It was a clearer hearing than with my ears. I trust that sense more than I trust my own ears. So I went towards it, and I thought I must be dying."

Pam felt herself drifting away from the operating room. The sounds and sights of the surgery faded, and she sensed herself moving beyond the walls. As she moved, a growing sense of detachment from her body took hold, as though something was leading her somewhere else. The atmosphere shifted, and she found herself in a space of peace and calm unlike anything she had ever known. A familiar voice called to her, and she realized it was her deceased grandmother. When asked how she first recognized it was her grandmother calling her, Pam explained, "I heard her voice. I was born with a unique inner ear, and I hear great voices, sounds, and tones. It was also my job. I remember very well the voice of my grandmother." Hearing her grandmother's familiar tone transported her back to childhood memories. "On hearing it, I remembered the time she called us for dinner when we were kids. It was the same thing."

Pam felt as though she were traveling through a tunnel. She described this sensation as deeply peaceful and comforting as if she were being embraced by warmth and love. "There was a sensation like being pulled, but not against your will," she remembered. "I was going on my own accord because I wanted to go." Pam used several metaphors to describe the unique experience. "It was like 'The Wizard of Oz,' being taken up in a tornado vortex, only you're not spinning around like you've got vertigo. You're very focused, and you have a place to go." She described the feeling as similar to a fast elevator lifting her upwards. "It was like a tunnel, but it wasn't a tunnel," she explained. The tunnel appeared as a dark shaft with a small, brilliant point of light at the end, which grew steadily larger and brighter as Pam moved toward it. The light was incredibly bright, so much so that she instinctively lifted her hands to shield her eyes. But when she looked, she couldn't see her hands. "But I knew they were there," she explained. "Not from a sense of touch. Again, it's terribly hard to explain, but I knew they were there."

As Pam reached the end of the tunnel, she encountered a presence she called 'the light'. But this was far more than mere light. It was consciousness and intelligence, a living presence that seemed to hold enormous wisdom. Pam quickly realized that the light was communicating with her, not through words or sound, but by directly sending emotions and understanding into her mind. At that moment, Pam felt herself expand. It was as if her awareness stretched out and merged with everything around her and she found herself in a timeless place filled with a deep sense of peace and understanding.

Though Pam had no particular interest in religion before her near-death experience, she felt certain she was now in the presence of something divine. Several beings of light appeared. At first, their shapes were blurry and hard to make out. But slowly, the figures became clearer, and Pam realized who they were: her loved ones who had passed away. Seeing their familiar faces filled her with comfort.

Her grandmother and uncle reassured her that everything was all right. Pam questioned her worthiness to be in this place, admitting, "I told myself that I did not deserve to be there because I was not someone perfect." Her grandmother's response was reassuring laughter. Though they didn't communicate with words, Pam understood her grandmother's thoughts. "She told me I was like a child who is sent to school," she recalled. "They were proud of me and that I deserved to be in their presence." Pam described her grandmother's appearance as youthful and vibrant, unlike the elderly woman she remembered. "I was very surprised when I saw her because she was not the same," Pam said. "When she died, she was old, but there she didn't seem to be old. I did not expect to see her so well." Pam was surprised to see her aunt among the gathering of loved ones, as she believed her aunt was still alive. It wasn't until after the operation that Pam learned her aunt had passed away while she was in the hospital.

"Everyone I saw, looking back on it, fit perfectly into my understanding of what that person looked like at their best during their lives," Pam recalled. "I recognized a lot of people. My uncle Gene was there. So was my Great-Great-Aunt Maggie, who was really a cousin. On Papa's side of the family, my grandfather was there." These loved ones were there to watch over her. What struck Pam most was their appearance. "They were clothed in light," she explained. "They looked like human beings, but unlike us. They were beings of light, each with different tones." Each figure seemed to radiate a unique glow.

Curious about the radiant light surrounding them, Pam asked if it was God. The surrounding figures responded, replying, "No." Pam noted, "It seemed to amuse them." They explained that the light was "what happens when God breathes," this light was not God itself but a manifestation of divine energy. Pam described the place where this occurred as a kind of waiting room between Earth and paradise, a place filled with a life-giving energy that seemed to restore her.

They told her she wouldn't be able to stay much longer and explained that if she ventured fully into the light, they could no longer guide her back to her body. "You would have gone too far," they said, meaning that her spirit and body could not reconnect. "I knew I was going to return to our world," she recalled. "I did not want to, but I think I had already made the choice before I even got there because I had children and a husband, and it was not time for me." She felt she had made the decision to return long before this experience.

An incredible energy radiated from her deceased relatives, an energy that healed her. "The only way I can explain it is something sparkly," she said. "Sparkles is the image that comes to mind." As they surrounded her, she felt waves of this sparkling energy washing over her, strengthening her from within. "I clearly remember the feeling of being nurtured and made strong," Pam said.

The experience drew to a close as her uncle guided her back toward her body. When she returned to the operating room, the sight of her body shocked her. She saw it as a "train wreck," a lifeless and terrible shell and she didn't want to look at it. Seeing her body in this state brought doubts to her mind about returning. Knowing her children would be well cared for, her husband could manage without her, and her strong mother would cope with her loss, she began to rethink her decision.

Pam recalled hearing the defibrillator being used on her twice. The first time, she only heard the sound, but on the second occasion, she actually saw the medical team using it on her body. "What surprised me the most that day is that they had music in the operating room," she said. "I didn't know that was done." Amid the intense atmosphere, she recognized the song playing in the background, "Hotel California" by the Eagles. The lyrics, "You can check out any time you like, but you can never leave," stood out to her. "I thought it was terrible," Pam recalled. "So insensitive." In the context of her near-death experience, the song's lyrics felt ironic.

"Then my uncle asked me to return to my body. He told me it was like jumping into a pool, but I did not want to. I was afraid it would hurt, and I did not want to return. So he told me, 'Do not you want to see your children? Do you not love your husband? And my sister, your mother?'" At that moment, Pam's uncle intervened. "Then he pushed me," she remembered. "I felt a definite repelling and, at the same time, a pulling from the body. The body was pulling, and the tunnel was pushing." The experience was intensely jarring, like "diving into a pool of ice water." She had a sensation of cold and discomfort accompanied by an aching in her chest as she merged back with her physical form. Pam's re-entry to her body was anything but gentle. The warmth, light, and love she had experienced seemed to fade, replaced by the heaviness of physical existence.

Once Pam had recovered enough from the operation to share her experience, her family initially dismissed it as mere hallucinations, finding the entire situation somewhat amusing. "That made everyone laugh, with the exception of the nurses, the doctor, the anesthesiologist, and the neurophysiologists," she noted. "They did not seem to find it funny and hardly dared to look at me."

Her medical team's reaction was telling. The professionals in the room were visibly unsettled, aware that Pam's account defied conventional explanation. "In fact, they knew that I was not hallucinating and that this had occurred. They had never heard of such things before." Pam herself doubted, wondering if it had just been a vivid dream or imagination. However, her medical team reassured her that the events she described matched the reality of what had happened during her surgery. Her descriptions of specific moments and details she could not have otherwise known made it clear to them that something truly extraordinary had taken place.

When asked if she feared death, Pam replied emphatically, "No! Are you kidding? I am more afraid of living! Dying is nothing. It's easy; living is hard."

Verification Events

Leg Artery

The surgical team needed to access an artery in Pam's leg to achieve the precise blood flow required for the heart-lung machine. During the procedure, Pam recalls hearing a voice say, "Her arteries and veins are too small," followed by Dr. Spetzler's response, "Use the other side." After the surgery, it was confirmed that this conversation had indeed taken place, and the team had switched to the other leg to secure the blood flow.

Pam couldn't have physically heard this exchange, even if her brain had been active. Prior to Dr. Spetzler's comment, she had molded earphones placed in her ears, which emitted loud, continuous clicking sounds. The doctor had set the clicking rate to 11.3 clicks per second and the volume to 95dB, equivalent to the sound level of a hand-held circular saw at a one-meter distance. Dr. Spetzler himself confirmed, "The molded speakers in her ears themselves, let alone the 95dB clicks, would have made it impossible for her to hear ordinarily, even if she had been fully conscious at that moment." This observation left the medical team astonished. Pam's ability to recount such specific details of the conversation, despite the physical barriers, was something they could not explain through any ordinary sensory perception.

The Saw

Pam recalled seeing Dr. Spetzler pick up a uniquely shaped saw to cut into her skull. "The saw-thing that I hated the sound of looked like an electric toothbrush," she explained. "It had a dent in it, a groove at the top where the saw appeared to go into the handle, but it didn't." She noted the saw came with interchangeable blades, which were stored in what looked like a socket wrench case. Pam vividly remembered the sound of the saw starting up. "I heard the saw crank up," she said. "I didn't see them use it on my head, but I think I heard it being used on something. It was humming at a relatively high pitch, and then all of a sudden it went 'Brrrrrrrrr!' like that." Her ability to describe the saw in such detail, along with the distinctive sound it made, was extraordinary, particularly given her physical state during the operation. The resemblance she noted to an electric toothbrush, complete with grooves, and the saw's distinct, intermittent hum added specificity that was impossible to attribute to hallucination or imagination. The saw was not visible when entering the operating room and was not removed from its container until an hour after the operation had started.

16. The Guardian and the Waiting Room of Souls

DAVID WALLACE

That David's heart had stopped while he was being resuscitated implies that his brain activity would have likely flatlined as well. Yet, as with other Near-Death Experiencers, he reported observing events from a perspective outside his body, details he couldn't have known through ordinary senses.

*

David Wallace was born on the Hawaiian island of Molokai, often regarded as the most spiritual island in the Hawaiian chain. During his life, he has had four Near-Death Experiences: the first at age 5, the second at 25, the third at 53, and the most recent at 57.

I'll be describing the second and fourth NDEs since they have verification events.

Second NDE

When David was 25, he had his second near-death experience while working as a police officer on Molokai, where he administered driving tests. The director of licensing from Maui had asked him to attend a week-long licensing seminar at Northwestern University in Chicago, and David agreed. Upon his arrival, he was met with frigid temperatures and 21 inches of snow. Having traveled from Hawaii, he had not expected such cold temperatures and hadn't brought proper winter clothing. He walked the half-mile from his hotel to the university each day, eventually catching a cold. By the time he returned to Hawaii, the cold had intensified, and he had to take time off work. A doctor later diagnosed him with double pneumonia and prescribed antibiotics. Although David was at home for three days, he showed no signs of improvement. "One night, despite taking all the cold drinks that I could drink and giving myself an ice bath, the fever continued," He said. "I couldn't fight it. I couldn't fight this anymore. I felt really depressed. I told my wife, 'I feel like I'm going to die.'" David went to bed and quickly drifted into a deep sleep.

David awoke, confused by the sensation of someone tugging at his toe. He realized his fever was gone, his breathing was normal, and he felt wonderful. His friend Bruce was at the foot of his bed. "He was dressed in a blue coverall like a mechanic would be wearing. I jump out of my bed, and I run up to him, and I hug him, and I call him by his name." David was so happy to see his friend that, at first, he didn't notice the problem. "Then suddenly I realized something was wrong with this picture because my friend Bruce had died about a year before that. So I pushed away. I said, 'Hey, Bruce, you're dead, right?'"

Bruce laughed and replied that, yes, he was dead.

David asked him, "Does this mean I'm there too?"

"David, no worry, you're okay," Bruce replied.

Looking at the bed, David noticed his own body lying there. "I felt really depressed," he said. "I sat down on the ground and started crying." Just then, he heard laughter. It was Bruce, who began teasing him, saying, "Come on, stop it already. You know you're not dead." Bruce said he'd been sent to show him something and offered a hand to help him up. Together, they walked to the closet, where Bruce opened the door and pushed the clothes aside. Instead of the back wall, there was a long, dark tunnel stretching deep into the distance. "At the other end of the tunnel," David recalled, "was this tiny, tiny speck of light."

As the two men walked further along the tunnel, the light grew brighter, and David noticed that both he and Bruce were now dressed differently. "Our clothes had changed into these soft, white garments that reminded me of feathers, delicate and soft," David said. "When I ran my hands over the fabric, it gave off an electric charge that made my hair stand up." When they reached the end of the tunnel, David saw a membrane over the exit that reminded him of a bubble gum bubble. Beyond the membrane lay a stunning landscape, where the colors of the grass, trees, and sky were extraordinarily vibrant and rich. As the light touched him, David felt a profound sense of love and welcome wash over him.

A group of people approached and David soon recognized some of their faces. "These were relatives who had passed away," he said. "My uncles, both of my grandparents, they were all there, coming close to the membrane at the tunnel's end." As David gazed at his family, he noticed animals nearby, and soon, several of his deceased pets bounded through the group to greet him. "My very first dog, Spotty, a little black-and-white dog, was there," David recalled, "and my pigeon, Wheezy, whom I had raised. They were all so loving. I could feel the love. It was overwhelming." Overcome with a desire to join them, David took a step forward. But Bruce raised an arm, blocking his path. At that moment, David's paternal grandfather looked at him and slowly shook his head, as if to say, "No, it's not your time to cross."

At that moment, David was startled to hear his daughter's voice calling out to him from the opposite side of the tunnel, "Daddy, where are you, Daddy?" He realized he couldn't go forward and needed to return to his daughter and his life. In an instant, he was swiftly moving backward through the tunnel as if some unseen force was pulling him. When he opened his eyes, he was in bed, and his fever had broken. "I told my wife about the NDE, and we decided to check the closet," David recalled. "When we opened it, the clothes inside were pushed aside."

Fourth NDE

In 2010, David was working as a teacher and believed he was in good health despite living with type 1 diabetes. But then, over a short period, he experienced three episodes of severe heart pain. The pain was intense, but David didn't collapse, and he assumed low blood sugar had caused it. However, his wife wasn't convinced, and she insisted he get a check-up.

David visited the doctor, and the results were unnerving. He had congestive heart failure. It was a serious condition that required immediate action. Doctors admitted him to the hospital and scheduled a triple bypass and mitral valve replacement surgery. The medical team prepared him and put David under anesthesia.

"I woke up in a deep, deep, dark place," he later explained. Suddenly, he felt a strong pulling sensation, and moments later, he found himself in a bright space, floating above the operating room. From this vantage point, David could see the doctors and nurses working intently. They moved quickly; their focus fixed on the patient lying on the table. At first, David didn't realize who the patient was. "I thought, whoever this person is, they're having a tough time," he recalled.

The team were using defibrillator paddles to resuscitate the patient. "I saw the paddles where they try to resuscitate you and get your heart started, and they're using the paddles, pom, pom, pom, pumping, and the body was jolting all over the place," he said. "So as I got closer, and I finally saw my face, I realized, oh, that's me. That's me on a gurney," David panicked. As soon as the fear set in, he felt something grab him from behind. He turned and saw a figure he recognized. It was Kupuna, the same guardian who had appeared during a near-death experience he'd had as a child. "He was there to calm me down," David said. "He knew I was afraid." The guardian pulled David away from the scene and the next thing he knew, he was above the hospital with downtown Honolulu below him. This familiar sight helped him feel more grounded. "I recognized the place, and it made me feel less scared," he said.

Things moved quickly. David traveled through a twisting, narrow tunnel. When he emerged, he was in a small room that felt strangely familiar. It was the same place he had visited during his first near-death experience at the age of five. The room reminded him of a security booth near a gate. It was just big enough for a few people. Inside were his guardian and three large Hawaiian men. They stood around him, watchful and protective. In his first NDE, Kupuna explained that this room was a kind of waiting room in between life and the afterlife. He also told David he was one of his ancestors.

Outside the room, through small windows, David saw people calling to him. They held up food and drinks, trying to tempt him. Feeling very hungry, David tried to move toward them, but the three men blocked his path. He pushed and fought against them, even kicking in frustration. But they didn't let him through. Exhausted, he finally stopped. His guardian turned to him and asked, "Are you finished now?"

Kupuna then gave him simple guidance. "Close your eyes and look again, but this time, use your spiritual eyes." When David followed the instruction, the truth became clear. The people outside the room were not kind or welcoming. They were hideous, frightening figures. "Do they want to take my soul?" David asked. "Yes," the guardian replied. "That's why we're here, to protect you," Kupuna explained that David's body was in serious trouble. They had brought him to this safe place until his fate became clear. Kupuna said, "You'll know soon." He reassured David, telling him he was proud of how David had been growing and using his natural talents and abilities. Slowly, David felt himself being pulled back and he woke up in the hospital's recovery room.

Because there were complications, the surgery had lasted seven hours instead of the expected four. As David recovered, he noticed something unusual. There were round, burn-like marks running down his ribs on both sides. When his wife arrived, he asked her to check his back. She confirmed the marks extended there too.

Verification Events

2nd NDE Verification

In this NDE, David's deceased friend Bruce had reached into the closet and pushed the clothes aside. After regaining consciousness from the NDE, he and his wife discovered the clothes had indeed been moved to the side of the closet.

4th NDE Verification

During his operation, David had watched the medical team trying to resuscitate him using the defibrillator. The circular burn marks on David's body were from the paddles used to restart his heart.

David said, "But later on, there was a nurse that was in the procedure that was actually related to me. She told me that the marks that I had, the circular marks, were from a specific instrument they used to try to restart my heart because they had to stop my heart to open it up and repair this valve they needed to work on. So they tried to restart the heart, and the heart just wouldn't go."

That David's heart had stopped while he was being resuscitated implies that his brain activity would have likely flatlined as well. Yet, as with other Near-Death Experiencers, he reported observing events from a perspective outside his body, details he couldn't have known through ordinary senses. The events he described were accurate.

Reference

David J. Wallace (2020) *The Journey of Our Souls: What You Can Learn From One Man's Multiple Near-Death Experiences'*, Aviva Publishing

17. A Sleeper Who Saw Everything

ANDREW ELKAN

Andrew's friend, Tyson, confirmed that he had sneaked into Andrew's ICU room, only to be promptly caught by hospital staff. Andrew could describe this incident in detail, even though he was in a coma at the time.

*

Andrew Elkan was born in Saint Louis, Missouri, where he spent his early years. In 1977, he moved to California, eventually settling in San Diego, where he began working as a veterinary assistant.

On the day of his near-death experience, his neighbor, a nurse, was startled by sounds of distress coming from his apartment above. Concerned, she dialed 911. The police arrived and knocked on Andrew's door, but there was no response. Following protocol, they knew that entering without permission would be unlawful, so they did not go inside. They also prevented the ambulance crew from entering, leaving Andrew without immediate help. After twenty minutes, a neighbor entered Andrew's apartment through a back window and opened the front door, giving emergency personnel access. Before paramedics could attend to Andrew, the police took charge, conducting a safety check first. When they noticed Andrew's tattoos, they became suspicious, assuming he might be involved in gang activity, and began searching the apartment for firearms and narcotics.

This added delay kept the paramedics waiting for another twenty minutes before finally receiving permission to enter. By then, forty minutes had passed since their arrival, and Andrew's condition had deteriorated. They found him in status epilepticus, a state of continuous, life-threatening seizures, which had caused significant brain swelling. Paramedics quickly transported Andrew to the nearest hospital, just five minutes away. To halt the seizures and reduce the severe brain swelling, the medical team placed him in an induced coma. After 24 hours, they carefully began the process of waking him. However, as soon as they gave him the medication, Andrew immediately began seizing.

Similar complications arose with every attempt to wake him, and his condition continued to worsen. Eventually, the medical staff informed his parents that Andrew was showing no response to any stimuli, a sign of profound neurological damage. With a heavy heart, they explained that although they could continue providing supportive care to keep him comfortable, the outlook was grim. The team advised Andrew's parents to consider other options, including end-of-life care, given his declining state and lack of response.

*

During this critical time, Andrew stood beside his hospital bed, watching the events. Although he couldn't hear anyone speaking, he somehow understood what was being communicated around him. He watched as his family members, defying ICU rules that permitted only family visitors, occasionally brought in friends. Andrew observed when the staff caught his friend Tyson and quickly asked him to leave. Andrew also saw the minor acts of care provided by his family. He noticed that when his lips became dry, his brother would carefully apply Vaseline. Even though he was in a coma, he experienced these moments from a perspective outside his body, aware of everything happening.

As time went on, Andrew's veins collapsed, and the medical team decided he needed a stent inserted to ensure continued treatment. Though still in a coma, Andrew consciously followed his body as they transported him down the hallway. "I remember the entire process of moving down the hallway and then being in the room," he later recalled. He watched the procedure in detail, noting the use of what appeared to be an X-ray or some type of CT scan to guide the placement of the stent. He could see everything, observing medical equipment and the procedure itself as though fully awake. The experience left him with a vivid memory of the process. During the procedure, Andrew saw that two medical personnel were involved. One stayed with him in the room while the other monitored the process from a separate area. While the stent insertion was underway, Andrew saw that one of his lungs was accidentally punctured. Fortunately, the puncture was small, and they completed the procedure without further problems.

"My parents were never informed about it," Andrew later recalled. "When I got out of the hospital, I was the one who brought it to their attention, and it was noted in the medical record." His memory of the incident, despite being in a coma, was so clear that he could recount details his family hadn't known and which had been documented only in the hospital records.

During his experience, Andrew repeatedly found himself in a vast space unlike anything he had ever known, filled with a sense of oneness with the universe. In this state, he felt a connection with everything around him. "There were moments when I was at a great distance," he recalled, "and other times when I was just in the room."

The day before he finally woke up, his parents, each of different faiths, one Christian and the other Jewish, arranged for a priest to administer the last rites while a rabbi offered a prayer for his healing. Andrew watched all of this from his out-of-body viewpoint, feeling more alive than his family could imagine. "I was watching all of this and thinking, 'hey, what do you think you're doing? I'm not dying,'" he recalled. The scene unfolded before him as he stood beside his own body. "It wasn't as if I was debating it. I was just next to myself, observing everything." He thought the situation was amusing, feeling fully present, watching his family's concern and faith-based efforts to cover all grounds.

After 28 days in a coma, Andrew finally regained consciousness, finding himself in a hospital bed. In a moment of confusion, he instinctively pulled out his endotracheal tube and

IV. Alarms immediately sounded, and the medical staff rushed in, quickly restraining him to stop him from injuring himself.

Andrew's journey to recovery was only beginning. He remained in the hospital for an additional five months, receiving intensive occupational and physical therapy. His coma had led to significant muscle atrophy, and he had to relearn basic functions, including how to walk and write. Despite making big strides in his recovery, Andrew has not fully regained his pre-coma abilities. He continues to face cognitive challenges, including issues with short-term memory. Throughout his coma, his brain had been in a vegetative state, and medical professionals had prepared his family for the likelihood that he would not recover. His remarkable journey back to consciousness defied expectations, given his brain's 28 days of inactivity.

Reflecting on his near-death experience, Andrew shared, "Looking back on it, it felt more like a night's sleep, yet it also seemed like lifetimes had passed. One thing I try to emphasize," he continued, "is that what happened was so far beyond a typical human experience, you can't come back and remember all of it or explain most of it."

Verification Events

Andrew's experience is notable for several verified details he observed while his brain was in a vegetative state.

Friend's Visit.

Andrew's friend, Tyson, confirmed that he had sneaked into Andrew's ICU room, only to be promptly caught by hospital staff. Andrew could describe this incident in detail, even though he was in a coma at the time.

Brother's care.

Andrew accurately recounted that his brother applied Vaseline to his lips to prevent dryness, an action his brother later confirmed.

Surgical Incident.

During the procedure of inserting a stent, the surgeon accidentally punctured one of Andrew's lungs. Although Andrew's parents were not informed, medical records and doctors later verified the incident, aligning with Andrew's memory of the event.

Religious Visit.

Andrew saw a priest administering the last rites and a rabbi offering a prayer for healing, which his parents later confirmed had occurred.

Conclusion

These verified events suggest Andrew experienced consciousness beyond physical brain activity, raising intriguing questions about how awareness might exist independently of the brain's typical functioning, especially during periods of clinical inactivity or coma.

18. The Surgeon's Dance and the Light Beyond

AL SULLIVAN

This detail caught Dr. LaSala's attention because it was a distinctive gesture, and Al couldn't have seen it under normal circumstances.

*

On the morning of January 18, 1988, 56-year-old Al Sullivan started his day like any other. As a delivery driver, he was preparing for his shift at the depot, ready to head out on his usual route. But an intense chest pain suddenly interrupted his routine. His coworkers, familiar with his history of heart problems, wasted no time and rushed him to the hospital. Soon after they arrived, doctors quickly began running tests to evaluate the condition of his heart. As they worked, one of Al's coronary arteries became completely blocked. The medical team decided that an urgent quadruple bypass surgery was Al's only chance of survival. During the operation, as the surgeons worked to restore blood flow, his heart suddenly stopped, and Al entered a state of clinical death.

At that moment, Al felt himself leave his body and begin moving upward into a thick, black, billowing smoke. "The smoke seemed to surround me no matter which way I turned," he later said. Eventually, he arrived at the edge of what appeared to be an amphitheater, though a large wall stood between him and the space beyond. An intensely radiant light glowed from behind the wall.

As he approached, three human-shaped beings of light materialized on his left. Their presence radiated warmth and familiarity, though they remained silent. When Al peered over the wall, he saw his own body lying motionless on an operating table below, draped in blue surgical sheets, his chest exposed. He saw his heart resting on a small glass table nearby, separate from his body. "I could see my surgeon," Al recalled, "the same one who had explained the procedure to me just moments earlier. He looked a little puzzled and was flapping his arms, almost like he was trying to fly." As Al watched the scene unfold, he recognized one of the spiritual beings standing beside him. It was his deceased brother-in-law.

To his lower right, Al noticed a tunnel filled with a brilliant yellow light. "The light from the tunnel was a golden yellow hue," he later said. "It was the brightest light I had ever seen, yet it didn't hurt my eyes at all." As he watched, a figure in a brown cloak floated gracefully through the tunnel, and Al felt an overwhelming feeling of love and peace. He immediately recognized the figure. It was his late mother, who had passed away when he was only seven years old. He was surprised by how youthful and vibrant she looked.

His mother's expression became serious, and she turned toward the surgeon. Al watched as she moved close to him and gently guided his hand to the left side of his heart. The surgeon reacted by making a sweeping motion, almost as if brushing away a fly. His mother turned back, reaching out toward him. Al tried to touch her hand, but he found himself unable to grasp it. She gave him one last smile, full of reassurance and love, before floating back into the tunnel. In the next instant, Al was back in his body.

Verification Events

It's important to understand that at the beginning of Al Sullivan's operation, the surgeons taped his eyes shut and positioned his head behind surgical drapes. These drapes completely blocked any view of the surgical team or the procedure. This layout made it impossible for Al to see what was happening during the surgery or to observe the actions of the medical staff.

Dr. Takata's movements

When Al woke up, he immediately shared with his cardiologist, Dr. Anthony LaSala, the detailed events he had witnessed during his surgery. At first, Dr. LaSala was skeptical and suggested that Al's experiences might have been hallucinations caused by the anesthesia or other medications. However, Al described a specific, unusual movement made by Dr. Hiroyoshi Takata during the procedure, how Dr. Takata had moved his elbows in a peculiar way. This detail caught Dr. LaSala's attention because it was a distinctive gesture, and Al couldn't have seen it under normal circumstances. When asked how he knew about it, Al firmly insisted that he had seen it himself, explaining that he had observed the surgery from a position above the operating room.

Medical equipment

Al described seeing a specific surgical instrument being used during his operation, one he had never encountered before. He gave a detailed account of the tool, including its shape and function. His description perfectly matched the instrument the surgical team had used on his body during the procedure. The most striking part of Al Sullivan's account is the level of detail in his observation. The instrument he described was a specialized tool used only in heart surgery, something he could not have seen or known about before. Because of his position on the operating table, even if he had been awake, his view would have been completely blocked by the drapes placed across his neck.

Despite these physical barriers, Al accurately described the instrument, including details about its backside, something not visible even to those casually familiar with surgical tools. The surgical team later confirmed that his description was incredibly precise, matching the actual instrument used during the procedure.

Al recounted that during the surgery, one nurse became upset when a piece of equipment malfunctioned. He remembered her exact words and described her body language as she reacted to the problem. Later, when he shared this, the nurse confirmed that the equipment had indeed failed and that her response matched Al's description.

VERIFIED NEAR DEATH EXPERIENCES

Conversation

Al described conversations that took place among the medical team during his surgery, even though he was in a state of clinical death with no detectable brain activity. He described hearing the surgeon and nurses discussing complications, including the malfunctioning equipment and the steps they took to resolve issues during his cardiac arrest. After his recovery, Al repeated these conversations in detail, recalling specific moments and decisions made during the surgery. The surgical staff later confirmed Al's account, saying it accurately matched what they said in the operating room.

Dr Bruce Greyson's research

In 1997, Dr. Bruce Greyson, a professor of Psychiatric Medicine at The University of Virginia, interviewed Al about his near-death experience (NDE). Dr. Greyson wanted to understand exactly when Al saw Dr. Takata's unusual arm movements, so he asked Al what else he noticed at that moment. Al described seeing his chest held open by clamps while two surgeons were working on his leg. This confused him, as he didn't understand why they would be operating on his leg when the problem was with his heart.

Dr. Greyson explained that the surgeons had been removing a vein from his leg to use as a graft for his heart, which was a standard part of the bypass surgery. This confirmed that Al was under general anesthesia and unconscious at the time he observed Dr. Takata waving his arms.

To verify Al's account, Dr. Greyson met with Dr. Takata and reviewed the details. Dr. Takata confirmed that Al's descriptions were accurate, including the specific surgical procedures and his own actions during the operation. This provided powerful support for the validity of Al's out-of-body experience, as he had no physical way of witnessing these events.

Conclusion

Al Sullivan's near-death experience (NDE) is one of the most compelling cases of veridical perception, where someone provided accurate and verifiable information about events occurring while he was clinically dead. Despite having no detectable brain activity, Al could describe the actions and expressions of the medical staff, overhear specific conversations, and even identify surgical instruments he had never encountered before and could not have seen from his physical position on the operating table. This case challenges conventional understandings of consciousness, as Al's perceptions during clinical death suggest an awareness independent of brain function.

Reference

Journal of Scientific Exploration, Vol. 12, No. 3, pp. 377±406, 1998.

19. Three Souls I Would Know

CRYSTAL FAITH

"I made them both believers with my ability to recall so much vivid detail of what I witnessed and heard them say," Crystal explained. Her descriptions left them with little doubt that what she experienced was real.

*

In 2000, Crystal Faith faced a challenging pregnancy, marked by pre-term labor that kept her in the hospital for 20 weeks. For the last 10 weeks, doctors worked to manage her labor, giving her medication to stop the contractions and keep the pregnancy stable. After another stay in the hospital, Crystal was finally ready to go home. However, before being discharged, she had a strong feeling that something wasn't right. Trusting her intuition, she asked to stay one more night.

The next morning, Crystal went into active labor. Her contractions were steady, but as the hours passed, her labor wasn't progressing as expected. The doctors decided to use a head monitor to check the baby's stability. This procedure required breaking the amniotic sac, a delicate and complicated process. Unfortunately, during the procedure, the doctor accidentally cut into a vein, leading to an amniotic fluid embolism. This condition occurs when amniotic fluid enters the mother's bloodstream, which can be life-threatening.

As Crystal's condition worsened, the baby's heart rate suddenly dropped, and Crystal struggled with her breathing. The medical team quickly reacted, with the anesthesiologist administering an epidural to help ease her pain and calm her down. "They had no idea why I was saying I couldn't breathe, except maybe they thought the contractions were too much for me," Crystal later explained. "So they were hoping to bring me some peace of mind." Just as the epidural took effect, a doctor rushed into the room to check on Crystal's condition. He explained that they needed to perform an emergency C-section because the baby's heart rate was dangerously low. The anesthesiologist pointed out that the epidural hadn't fully worked yet, so if they proceeded immediately, Crystal would likely experience significant pain during the surgery.

The doctor turned to 17-year-old Crystal and asked, "Do you want your baby alive or dead?" Crystal agreed to go ahead with the C-section. "So I'm lying there, and I feel paralyzed," she recalled. "My mouth feels dry, like cotton, and I can't move, but I feel everything." Her lungs began filling with fluid, and Crystal's body struggled to get enough oxygen. Eventually, her heart stopped. "I coded on the C-section table," she said. At that moment, Crystal felt herself lift away from her body. She was now above, looking down at the scene below. Alarms blared as medical staff rushed around, trying to save her.

"I hovered down into the room to look at this machine," she recalled. "I remember thinking, wow, okay, so this machine is showing me I'm flat-lined, and I know that's me on the table, but I honestly didn't care at all about what I looked like or seeing my own body." A doctor entered the room, followed by a group of medical students who had come to observe what they thought would be a routine C-section. The doctor, who had recently covered amniotic fluid embolism in his lectures, quickly recognized the signs of this rare complication and called out the diagnosis.

The medical team immediately shifted their focus to resuscitating Crystal and addressing the amniotic fluid embolism. Once her condition was stable, they began preparing to transfer her to the ICU. Knowing she needed specialized care, they requested a pulmonologist to accompany her during the transfer. From her out-of-body perspective, Crystal watched as the doctor stepped into the elevator with her gurney. She noticed he was wearing scrubs but not a surgical cap, and from above, she saw a bald spot on the top of his head.

Once in the ICU, the medical staff placed Crystal on a ventilator to help her breathe, but she felt trapped and confused and tried to stop them. At that moment, she felt herself leaving her body again. This time, she slipped out through the back of her head. "I was hovering. I felt like a ghost," she later recalled. From her viewpoint above, she could sense the emotions of the medical team. "I'm watching them work on my body in the ICU, and I can feel everything the doctors are feeling," she said. "They're sincere, they're passionate, they absolutely and clearly want me to survive." As she watched them working to revive her, Crystal felt calm and at peace. Despite the chaos below, she couldn't understand why they were so worried, as she felt everything was fine.

She noticed the spirit of a woman beside her. Crystal asked her, "Who are you?" The woman communicated telepathically. "I am the one that named you," the woman said. "I am so happy you are here, but I want you to see this first so you understand what is going on." Crystal felt a connection to the woman as if they had known each other their whole lives. Looking back on the encounter, Crystal later said, "I don't know if it was truly my maternal grandmother or if it was someone interdimensional presenting themself as my grandmother." In that space, Crystal felt that lying or deception wasn't possible, and she could accept the woman's words without hesitation.

Standing by the hospital window, Crytal's mother prayed as she stared out at a fierce blizzard. The streetlights cast an eerie orange glow on the falling snow. Crystal could feel her mother's thoughts and emotions as if they were her own and felt hurt and confused by her mother's silent prayer. "Okay, God, come in here and just take her." Crystal had always believed that a mother's love was based on hope, not on asking God to take her child. But as she heard her mother's prayer, she understood the weariness behind it. Her mother wasn't asking for death but for release from the pain of watching her daughter suffer.

The woman beside Crystal offered reassurance and helped her understand her mother's actions. She explained that her mother wasn't giving up hope but experiencing a form of surrender. Crystal tried to describe this process of communication. "I wish I had the right words. When you communicate telepathically, it's like receiving entire concepts, and there's no true language for it." Crystal continued, "So while 'surrendering' isn't quite the right term, it's the best I can find in our language to explain what's happening." She understood now that her mother's prayer wasn't about wanting to lose her but a deep letting go of control.

Crystal understood that when her mother passed away, she would become a complete, wise spiritual being, just as Crystal was at that moment. But while her mother was still alive in her physical body, her understanding was limited. The woman explained that only a small part of her mother's soul could reside in her body at any time. The human brain, with all its limitations, naturally dulled much of her awareness. This meant that her mother could not fully experience the depth of her true self while still living in the physical world.

Crystal floated out of the ICU to the hospital waiting room and saw her grandfather. A deep sense of connection washed over her. She could sense his thoughts and feel everything he was feeling. Crystal saw her sister, who worked in the hospital's admissions department, walk past with Crystal's X-rays in hand. She was on her way to deliver them to the attending physician but paused outside the waiting room to speak to their grandfather. As Crystal watched, she felt her sister's emotions as if they were her own. She later described the sensation: "So when she was walking past the waiting room, and she felt nervous and scared, I felt this feeling like you have fear in you, and I don't know why, it was overpowering fear."

Breaking hospital protocol, Crystal's sister took the X-rays out and showed them to their grandfather. He looked at the images, and her sister explained that Crystal's lungs were 85 to 90 percent filled with fluid. As Crystal watched, she saw her grandfather's face fall, and he fell back onto the pink sofa in the waiting room.

At that moment, the woman gestured for Crystal to turn and move toward the light. As Crystal turned, the warm, bright light surrounded her in an embrace of peace and love, and she felt she was the light, an inseparable part of its endless healing energy. Crystal heard the most beautiful music she had ever experienced. She was certain it was the singing of angels. "The sound was so beautiful and pure," she later recalled. Unlike earthly sounds that travel through sound waves, this music existed differently, unfiltered and direct, requiring no medium to carry it. Each angelic voice was distinct, like a beautiful instrument.

Yet, they blended together perfectly, forming a never-ending sea of music.

After some time, Crystal's curiosity grew, and she wondered what might lie beyond this peaceful space. The moment she thought about moving, something thrust her forward at an incredible speed. As time passed, Crystal felt the need to see color, and suddenly, bright and beautiful colors appeared around her, forming a stunning garden. "The colors just appeared everywhere, and I was surrounded by the most beautiful garden," she said. "The garden was made of color itself. People talk about it, but it's true. The colors were so bright and alive, nothing like what we see on Earth."

There was a deep sense of connection to everything around her. The plants, the colors, the shapes, all seemed to come from the same mind. It felt as if she was a part of the creation, helping to bring this place into being. While admiring a flower, she thought to herself, "I wonder what it would look like if it opened." At that moment, the flower bloomed. As she continued to take in the surroundings, small creatures, **similar to** fairies or butterflies, appeared around her. They came into view as soon as she thought of them. Crystal realized that with every thought, she was shaping the garden around her.

To her right, Crystal saw a peaceful courtyard. In the center, a man sat on a bench, his back to her. When he looked over, he smiled and invited her to join him. "So, of course, I went over and sat with him," she said. The man shared vast amounts of knowledge with Crystal. She felt the information was being "downloaded" directly into her mind. "It was too much to remember fully," she recalled. Over the years, bits and pieces of it have come back to her. The man also expressed his love and pride for her.

Curious, she asked him how he knew her so well. With a smile, he replied, "I've always been with you." At that moment, memories of her childhood filled Crystal's mind. She remembered times when she had felt lonely, playing with her imaginary friend. As she looked down, she was amazed to see herself sitting next to her younger self, as if time had no meaning here. Crystal suddenly realized that this man, who felt so familiar to her, might very well be her higher self. The man turned to Crystal, telling her it was time to move on to the next place. But before they left, he wanted her to see something. He gestured for her to look down at the space in front of them.

"When he motioned for me to look down, in this courtyard, there were these three little babies," Crystal recalled. "I remember thinking, wow, I didn't see them there before, but I hadn't thought to look for them." She sensed that the man had co-created this moment with her, intentionally bringing these three babies into her view. The sight of them felt important, as if each one represented something meaningful in her life or future. Crystal understood that this moment had been carefully planned and that these three little souls were significant in ways she would understand later. The babies wore glittering, shimmering gowns with what appeared to be halos that also resembled delicate little wings. They radiated an energetic presence and didn't have a distinctly masculine or feminine appearance.

"He told me; these are your future three babies that you would have had in that lifetime. But that's okay because you can have another chance with them. You'll get another opportunity to be their mother." Crystal looked into the eyes of one baby, amazed by its beauty, feeling a desire to pick it up and hold it close. But she didn't realize that her gaze had formed a telepathic connection. To her surprise, the baby responded with a firm voice, saying, "How dare you want to pick me up? I am my own wise, spiritual, divine being, just like you. You can't just pick me up without asking!" The response from the baby caught Crystal off guard. She had assumed the beings were innocent and childlike, but she quickly realized they had much more to them than she had imagined. These beings weren't simply children, they were fully aware spiritual entities.

The baby's unexpected reply unsettled Crystal, and in the blink of an eye, she was thrown into a vast, dark void. She knew immediately that this place was a creation of her own mind. In this space of total emptiness, she was stripped of everything: her memories, her identity, and any sense of context. It was as though someone had pressed a master reset button, and everything that made her who she was had been erased.

For what felt like a very long time, Crystal existed in a deep, black space. Even though the darkness around her felt full of information, it didn't push her to learn or do anything. It felt like a choice was being offered to her. But Crystal didn't feel the need to look for answers. Instead, she just accepted everything as it was and felt calm, content simply existing with no purpose or movement.

After an eternity in the void, Crystal awakened from her deep state of pure being. She felt herself expand, growing from just existing into something more, an "I am." Thoughts slowly formed within her, carrying a curiosity about what was ahead. She considered her potential in this space and wondered if she could create something just by using her mind. As soon as she thought of this, a sudden flash of lightning lit up her vision. "I could see like a lightning bolt or a surge of energy or an energy streak go across my plane of vision," Crystal recalled. "Which is really hard to explain because you can feel and sense everything there, but I see this energy spark and then I was thinking that was fun.

Then she wondered, "Okay, so what's next?" As soon as the thought crossed her mind, she became aware of time again. Memories of her life on Earth surfaced, and she suddenly realized, "Oh, I just had a lifetime!" Thinking about this, a sense of dread crept in. She remembered teachings of hell as a place of darkness, without love or light. "Am I in hell?" she wondered. The black void now felt ominous. As her fear grew stronger, Crystal called out to the universe, pleading for love and declaring her belief in God. "Please, I'm not meant for this. I believe in you," she cried out. In an instant, she found herself in a room filled with pure, radiant white light. Her panic melted away as warmth surrounded her, and even though she had no physical body, Crystal felt as if she were lying on a soft bed. For a moment, she wondered if she had somehow returned to the hospital.

"The light was so bright, and I was like, okay, am I back in the hospital room?" Crystal recalled. "Eventually, my eyes adjusted, and this interdimensional being came to the foot of my bed. I felt like it was an angel, but it was different. It was like a light being with so much light radiating from where its chakra system was in the back that it created the illusion of light wings, and the crown chakra had a light halo, just like an angel would look like."

Crystal felt an overwhelming urge to make eye contact. It dawned on her if she looked into the being's eyes, they could communicate telepathically. She had just come from a place she could hardly describe, a dark, empty void where she came to understand the flow of time and its endlessness. It was in that space she remembered she had just had a baby. More than anything, she wanted her baby with her. It wasn't that she was afraid, but she was filled with a sense of longing that was hard to describe. The feeling was similar to a frequency she was sending out, yet feeling at the same time.

At that moment, she was determined to connect. Crystal begged the being in front of her, pleading for them to look her in the eyes. The being tried to resist, signaling that it wasn't possible, but Crystal wouldn't give up. Finally, the being lowered their gaze, and when their eyes met, something extraordinary happened. The connection between them went beyond just a simple gaze. It was as if the being's eyes were also Crystal's.

"Eventually, she looked down at my eyes, and the moment our gaze met, the essence of her soul came through and literally zapped me backward with a rush of fear, energy, care, knowledge, and love," Crystal recalled. "I remember being filled with everything there is to know." Crystal pleaded with the light being to send her back to her body and insisted, "I need to be with my baby." But the being's response was uncompromising. "I can't send you back," it replied. "Your body is too damaged, and it can no longer support you."

The words hit Crystal hard. The truth of her situation became clear as she understood that returning to her earthly life, her child, and her loved ones might be impossible. Overcome with the thought of leaving her child behind, Crystal begged the being, "Please, send me back. Let me go back to my baby, and I promise I'll return to this place again with them. I just need to give them all the love I have."

The being said she could do more for her baby from the spirit realm than she ever could in the physical world. It showed her how her love could reach her child through others. The being explained that her love could influence people's thoughts, leading them to support and care for her child in ways she couldn't do herself. As the being communicated, countless images appeared before Crystal, showing how her love would continue to flow through the lives of those around her baby. Crystal longed to hold her baby, to bring her child into this peaceful space where they could be together. She wanted to experience life with her child, not just watch from afar.

Finally, Crystal realized her desire to return wasn't about herself but about her child. She needed to make sure her baby was safe and loved. The being seemed to understand her pain. "I want to help you," it said, "but I can't. I don't have permission." Crystal begged the being, asking it to at least try to seek permission. The being agreed and turned its gaze upward. As it did, beams of light shot out from its eyes. These beams of light seemed to carry something within them. Intricate patterns, like threads of information, weaved into the glow. These beams were carrying the being's request, mixed with her own deep longing to return. The light felt like it was reaching out to something higher, something with the power to grant permission.

Without warning, Crystal felt an intense surge of energy fill her entire being and she lifted slightly before gently settling back down. She could feel her physical form again, it felt weak and heavy, and she couldn't move. Her soul was back in her body.

The medical team had worked tirelessly for 45 minutes trying to revive Crystal, but eventually, they had to accept that their efforts were unsuccessful. They recorded her time of death and left the room, leaving only Crystal's mother and a nurse behind. But just eight minutes later, a sudden blip appeared on the heart monitor, a heartbeat. At that exact moment, Crystal's mother felt a powerful surge of energy pass through her. She dropped to her knees as if an unseen force had filled the room. The medical team quickly returned, rushing in to stabilize Crystal, now alive once more. Her condition was critical. The amniotic fluid had entered her bloodstream, affecting her heart, brain, and all her major organs, a condition that often leads to a fatal outcome. One doctor, trying to prepare Crystal's mother for the worst, warned that Crystal might have suffered severe brain damage due to the lack of oxygen and the widespread embolism.

Despite these grim predictions, Crystal showed signs of recovery, and after ten weeks of intensive care and many medical interventions, she started improving. Against all odds, she defied the initial outlook and eventually left the ICU, a recovery her medical team described as a miracle.

Verification Events

The Waiting Room

On the night Crystal was admitted to the hospital in critical condition, her sister, who worked in the admissions department, was on duty. In urgent cases, when a doctor orders an emergency X-ray, it must be hand-delivered to avoid delays in the hospital's tube system, which can take hours. Understanding how serious Crystal's condition was, her sister took the X-rays to the doctor's office, located just past the waiting room. On her way, she made a brief stop in the waiting room to show the X-rays to their grandfather. Though she knew it was against hospital rules, she wanted to keep the family informed.

Later, Crystal amazed her family by recounting, in vivid detail, everything that had happened in the waiting room while she was in the ICU. She described the events as she had been watching from above, looking down at the scene. Her grandfather, doubtful, suggested that maybe she had imagined it. To convince him, Crystal described the waiting room with remarkable accuracy, down to its decor and furnishings. "I described the wallpaper," she said. "It was 2002, so think mahogany, pink, green, very dated. You know, the kind of furniture and wallpaper you don't forget. I can still picture it clearly, and I had never been in that waiting room before." Her detailed description, including the layout and style of the room, matched perfectly, even though she had never physically entered the space. Crystal explained that she had seen it all during her out-of-body experience.

Crystal told her grandfather, "I saw you fall back onto that pink sofa, and I even felt the air from the cushions go 'pssh' as you sat down." Her grandfather replied, "You know, one of my most vivid memories from that moment is exactly that feeling of sitting back on the couch."

Crystal's sister and grandfather found her account impossible to dismiss. The level of detail she provided, from the decor of the room to the specific words spoken and emotions felt, was far too accurate to be a coincidence. "I made them both believers with my ability to recall so much vivid detail of what I witnessed and heard them say," Crystal explained. Her descriptions left them with little doubt that what she experienced was real. Beyond just witnessing events, Crystal had felt their emotions and this, along with her descriptions, validated the experience not only for Crystal but for her family as well.

The Spirit Woman

Six months after her near-death experience, Crystal was living with her mother as she continued her recovery. Late one night, she went to the kitchen to get a drink and found her mother browsing family history on a genealogy website. On the screen was an old photograph of several women sitting on a wall, dressed in 1950s-style clothing. "I remember looking at the picture and pointing right at the woman in the middle," Crystal recalled. "I said, 'Oh my gosh, I met her. I met her. That was the lady above the room!'"

Crystal's mother quickly explained that she couldn't have met the woman in the photo. "She died just before you were born," her mother said. But Crystal was certain. "She was the one who named me," Crystal insisted. "My mom just broke down. I had no idea why." After gathering herself, her mother admitted, "You're right. She did name you, and I never told anyone that." Her mother then shared a story from her pregnancy. When she was about eight and a half months along, her grandmother, the woman in the photo, had predicted the baby would be a girl and suggested the name Crystal Faith.

Reflecting on the experience, Crystal said, "It deepened her spiritual awareness. She realized her mother came to me during that experience to share a message with her from the afterlife."

The Pulmonologist

During Crystal's emergency C-section, having a pulmonologist present wasn't standard protocol. However, because of the severe fluid buildup in her lungs, one was called in. He arrived in such a rush that he didn't have time to put on his surgical cap. From her out-of-body perspective, Crystal noticed every detail, including his uncovered bald spot. Later, she told him, "You didn't have a hat on, and I saw your bald spot." The pulmonologist was visibly shocked. Crystal then went even further, accurately recounting the exact thoughts he'd had during that moment.

Later, the pulmonologist opened up to Crystal, sharing that he had been going through a very hard time. His wife was battling terminal cancer, and the stress had weighed heavily on him. Crystal's account of seeing him in the operating room and the elevator, despite the fact that she had been clinically dead, had a profound impact on him. Her story brought him a sense of calm and peace during a difficult period in his life. It touched him deeply, helping him cope with his struggles and giving him a new perspective on life and death.

"It made that time with her more meaningful for both of us," he said. Crystal's near-death experience not only changed her own life but also gave peace and understanding to someone going along his own difficult journey.

20. City of Light and Desert of Shadows

GEORGE RITCHIE

What he had witnessed in the spiritual realm had now taken form in the physical world, eight years later.

*

In September 1943, George Ritchie, an army medical student, started his basic training at Camp Barkeley, Texas. A few weeks later, in the cold December weather, George and his platoon had to sit outside for a two-hour lecture on cleaning equipment. Many of the men caught colds, and by the next morning, George was feeling sick. He went to the sick bay, where a thermometer showed he had a fever of 102 degrees. Worried about his condition, the medical staff sent him by jeep to the camp hospital, a large complex with 5,000 beds for the 250,000 men stationed at Camp Barkeley. Once there, the medical staff put George in the isolation ward so they could watch him closely.

The one thing on George's mind was his upcoming trip home to Richmond, Virginia, scheduled for December 18th. He was both desperate and excited to return home, as his medical training was set to begin in Richmond on December

22nd. As his illness worsened, he changed his train ticket to the 19th, hoping he'd recover in time.

He was temporarily released from the recuperation ward on December 18th and saw a movie, hoping to distract himself. But during the movie, a violent coughing attack overcame him. Worried that his condition might prevent him from making the train, George tried to hide how unwell he felt. The doctors prescribed him an APC pill, a combination of aspirin, phenacetin, and caffeine, to help ease his symptoms. After taking the medication, he dropped into a deep sleep.

George awoke around midnight, feeling an odd weakness in his legs as he attempted to get out of bed. His muscles trembled uncontrollably, and he was shocked to see that when he coughed, the sputum he spat into a cup had a tinge of blood. He borrowed a thermometer from the ward assistant, but his vision blurred, making it impossible to read. The assistant informed him that his temperature was 106.5 degrees. A nurse was quickly called and when she rechecked his temperature, she confirmed the dangerously high reading. Soon after, a doctor arrived, examined him, and ordered an immediate X-ray. In the X-ray room, George stood in front of the machine, but before the scan could proceed, his legs buckled beneath him. Overcome by the fever and weakness, he slipped into unconsciousness.

VERIFIED NEAR DEATH EXPERIENCES

George awoke with a start and checked for a clock, desperate not to miss his train home. But there was no bedside clock. Annoyed, he got out of bed and searched his small isolation cubicle, realizing with frustration that none of his belongings were there. Turning back toward the bed, he froze. Someone was lying in it, someone who looked disturbingly like himself.

Confused but focused on catching his train, George left the cubicle to find the ward assistant. He checked the supply room, but it was empty, and his clothes were nowhere to be found. Puzzled, he wandered down the corridor, noticing that the usually bustling ward was now eerily silent, with no staff in sight. Just then, he spotted a sergeant approaching, and George hurried to speak with him. But to his shock, the sergeant walked straight past, as though he was invisible. George realized that if he hadn't stepped aside, the sergeant would have walked right into him.

At the end of the corridor, George spotted an exit and decided to head to Richmond as quickly as possible. As soon as he made up his mind to leave, he found himself outside the building, moving over the landscape at an unbelievable speed, faster than he had ever moved before. Despite the freezing December air, he didn't feel the cold. Looking down, he was shocked to realize he was gliding above mesquite bushes. The world beneath him blurred as his speed increased, and soon, Camp Barkeley was far behind. He saw a dark, frozen river flash below, followed by a town with caution lights blinking at intersections. The dry desert landscape changed into snow-covered fields and forests, with more roads and dark towns passing beneath him. His speed far outpaced any train, and for a moment, he was certain he was on his way to Richmond.

However, as he sped onward, doubts crept in. Was he heading in the right direction? This strange journey defied all sense and reason, and George wondered if he had somehow taken a wrong turn. He slowed to a stop and hovered above a large bridge that stretched over a wide river, with a sprawling city visible on the far shore. As he looked down, George wondered if he could descend and ask someone for directions to Richmond. Without thinking twice, as if his thought had taken control, he descended and stopped fifty feet above a dimly lit street below. Beneath him was a one-story building with a red roof. Above the door, a sign read "Cafe," and a blue neon Pabst Blue Ribbon Beer sign lit up the front window.

He glanced down and saw a man hurrying toward the all-night cafe, lost in thought. George decided to ask him for help. With just a thought, he stood on the sidewalk beside him. The man, wrapped in a warm coat, walked on without noticing George, even as he kept pace beside him. George asked, "What city is this?" The man didn't respond. His eyes remained focused on the cafe door, unaware of George's presence. Growing frustrated, George reached out to tap the man's shoulder, but to his shock, his hand passed right through him, as if he were invisible or made of nothing at all. It was then that George fully understood the weight of his situation. He seemed to be in this place but without a physical body, unable to touch or be seen by the world around him.

George walked over to a telephone pole on the sidewalk, intending to lean against the guy wire for support. But, to his frustration, his hand slipped straight through it, as though he were made of air. As he reflected on his predicament, he realized that the man at the cafe hadn't seen or heard him, much like the sergeant hadn't back in the hospital. As he considered this, his mind wandered back to the figure he had seen lying in the hospital bed, the one that had looked so eerily like himself. Could it be that he had somehow become separated from his own body? The thought sent a rush of urgency through him, and without even trying, he moved back toward Camp Barkeley. This time, he traveled even faster, covering the distance in moments.

Before he knew it, he was standing in front of the hospital. Driven by a desperate need for answers, he hurried inside, determined to return to the isolation ward and see for himself if his body was still lying in that bed. After navigating several hallways, George finally found a ward with isolation cubicles, but none of the three contained his body. Panic rose as he launched into a frantic search through the sprawling, 5,000-bed hospital, scanning room after room in the dim, quiet light of night. He worried that, in the flesh, he might not even recognize himself, as he had only ever seen his face in the flat reflection of a mirror. To make matters worse, the hospital was filled with young men of similar age, height, and military haircuts, making his search even more overwhelming and difficult.

Then he realized he was wearing his Phi Gamma Delta ring, a unique marker that could help him identify his body. With renewed focus, George continued his search. Eventually, he made his way to the X-ray lab and spotted the technician he had spoken to earlier. He called out, shouting the man's name, but once again, he was ignored. Unfazed, George pressed on and finally came upon a small cubicle with a single, unmoving figure lying in the bed. The sheet covered the person's face, and the body lay still. Their arms rested outside the sheet, and as George leaned in closer, he saw it, the Phi Gamma Delta ring on the left hand. A sudden jolt of realization hit him. This was his body, motionless in the bed, lifeless.

He slumped down, trying to sit on the edge of the bed. But then, something unexpected happened. The light in the room grew brighter, not from the bedside lamp but from everywhere around him. The intensity of the light was so overwhelming that, had he been using his physical eyes, he was certain they would have been blinded. Slowly, the radiant light took form, shaping itself into the figure of a man. A voice resonated in his mind, clear and commanding, "Stand up." The authority in the voice was unlike anything George had ever felt. Without hesitation, he found himself on his feet, his body moving in response to the powerful presence before him. This spiritual being filled him with an overwhelming sense of peace and love.

The being of light showed George his entire life, each event unfolding in vivid detail. The small hospital cubicle remained, but now it felt as though a vast, three-dimensional panorama extended outward, surrounding him from every direction. Moments of joy, sorrow, and everything in between played out before him, thousands of scenes unfolding at once. Time seemed to lose all meaning, and it was as if he absorbed everything simultaneously.

In the background of every scene, a question echoed: "What did you do with your life?" At first, George thought this question was about measuring his achievements, and he started searching through the scenes, hoping to find something impressive. His eyes landed on the memory of achieving the rank of Eagle Scout. At that moment, George felt a brief surge of pride, but as he looked closer, an unsettling realization formed. The memory of achieving Eagle Scout was centered on his own accomplishment and the attention he received. Standing in the presence of this unconditional love and understanding, George saw that the question wasn't about his achievements at all. It was asking for something much deeper. How had he impacted others? How had he shown love, kindness, and compassion?

The surrounding scenes shifted, their meaning deepening. They invited him to look beyond pride and ego, urging him to reflect on the moments that truly defined his life. Moments of selflessness, care, and connection were the true measures of his journey. At that moment, George realized he was not being judged by this spirit. There was no judgment at all. Instead, he understood he was the one passing judgment on himself. As his life unfolded before him, George watched every moment with growing clarity. The question, "What did you do with your life?" arose once again. This time, its meaning was unmistakable. It was about love. The question invited George to reflect on how deeply and unconditionally he had loved. Had he shown love freely, without hesitation? Had he given, expecting nothing in return? Had he accepted others as the being of light accepted him now, with complete understanding and no conditions?

George and the being of light were swept from the hospital, rising quickly through the sky. As they ascended, he noticed a small, intense light in the distance, growing larger as they approached. The closer they got, the clearer it became that they were heading toward a city, a bustling hub of war production that seemed to never stop.

As they landed among the buildings and people, George saw crowds moving with a sense of purpose. But when he focused on the individuals, something strange caught his attention. Two men passed directly through each other, as if neither was aware of the other's presence. Curious, George looked around and soon realized he could see through the walls of the buildings. Inside, people were squeezed together, working tirelessly at machines or desks, completely absorbed in their tasks. There was no chatter, no interaction, just intense focus. The city was alive with relentless motion, but its people seemed unaware of one another, all caught in their singular drive to produce and fulfill a purpose.

As George watched, he saw a young man speaking into a machine, typing out a letter, while an older man stood behind him, angrily yelling at him. But the young man didn't seem to notice the older man at all. Nearby, a woman asked a man for a cigarette, but he didn't respond, as if she wasn't there. Frustrated, she reached for one, but her hand went straight through it. George thought back to the time outside the all-night cafe when he had tried to talk to the man on the street. He suddenly understood that these people were going through the same separation he had. They, too, were dead. The work and desires that had once been so important to them now trapped them, making them unaware of their true state or of others like them.

Moving quickly from one city to another, George watched as people went through endless, repetitive routines. In one place, he saw a young man following an older man through a house, constantly apologizing with a pained look on his face. The father, however, seemed completely unaware of his son's presence, ignoring his desperate pleas for forgiveness. Confused, George asked the being of light why the young man was so sorry. He could sense the weight of the answer. The young man had taken his own life, thinking that death would free him from his pain. But instead of escaping his torment, he was still trapped in it, unable to find peace.

George noticed a subtle but clear difference between the living and the dead. The living were surrounded by a faint, glowing aura, while the dead lacked this glow, looking more like dark shadows. He glanced down at himself and realized, to his shock, that he, too, lacked the bright aura of the living.

In a crowded bar, he watched sailors drinking heavily. Several dead men close by made efforts to join in and tried to hold the drinks in front of them. Their frustration was clear as their hands went through the glasses, unable to touch or taste the alcohol. Suddenly, one of the living sailors slumped over, overcome by his heavy drinking. As he did, his aura seemed to flicker and split open, creating a gap. In that instant, a non-living sailor leaped toward him, merging with his form. The two seemed to fuse, and where there had been two people, there was now only the one collapsed man. George felt a chill as he realized what he had just seen. The dead sailor had tried to possess the living man's body, hoping to experience the alcohol. These spirits were trying to relive sensations they could no longer feel by connecting with those whose light had grown dim. This desperation to experience the physical world gave George a deep understanding of the restless, unresolved nature of these spirits. He realized this place was a kind of hell where the dead lingered, bound to an earth they could see but never touch, trapped by their unresolved desires and bitterness.

George turned to the spiritual being and asked why they had brought him there to see this. In that instant, the being transported him to a vast open plain crowded with more of the dead, shuffling about in an atmosphere heavy with anger and misery. There were no living people among them. Many fought violently, gouging, biting, and hitting one another. Yet, despite their attacks, they caused no harm. Their hands passed through each other as if they didn't exist. As George watched, he noticed their thoughts and emotions seemed to take form around them. Shouts of "I warned you, but you wouldn't listen!" and "It was obvious I was better than you!" echoed in a chaotic noise of blame and resentment. Each soul seemed caught in a loop of judgment and a desperate need to prove themselves superior. This awful behavior and the sense of superiority struck a chord with George as he recognized the same behavior within himself. He realized that, if left unchecked, such behavior could lead to a state of self-inflicted torment.

He watched the tortured spirits, stuck in their misery without trying to leave. Though they could have walked away, he realized they believed there was no escape. Above the plain, George noticed figures of light bending over the anguished souls, speaking to them gently. These beings, filled with compassion, reached out with words of comfort and guidance, offering a path away from the torment. But the souls below seemed oblivious, unable to hear or acknowledge them. George realized that these beings of light had been there all along, their presence hidden not because they were invisible but because they were unseen by those full of anger and bitterness.

A veil lifted and George's perception suddenly changed. He saw a magnificent city that had always been present, hidden from his view until his mind was ready to see it. The city was awe-inspiring, its architecture surpassing the beauty of anything on Earth. The air felt alive, resonating with a vibrant, peaceful energy.

They entered a building, and George found himself in a hallway lined with many doors, each leading to a room bustling with activity. Figures in flowing, hooded robes moved quietly by, radiating a calm energy. Through open doors, George saw hooded figures poring over complex charts or working at intricate consoles with flickering lights. Though he had studied science in college, what he saw here was far beyond his understanding. He saw a massive metallic sphere, with people inside busy working on intricate mechanical devices.

This college was more than a place of learning; it was a space where knowledge and spiritual growth merged. George realized these beings were studying the universe itself, looking into science, philosophy, and wisdom far beyond human comprehension. As they continued their journey, George heard beautiful music, a sound so exquisite it was beyond anything he had heard on Earth. They soon entered an immense library. Shelves stretched endlessly, filled with works written on books, parchments, clay tablets, and leather scrolls.

From the library, they moved into an open void, a space that seemed to have no physical boundaries. In the far distance, George saw a radiant city of light. Its brilliance illuminated everything around it, with every surface shimmering. Glowing beings moved gracefully through its streets, exuding an aura of peace and wisdom. As George gazed at the city, two of the light beings began traveling toward him, moving at an unimaginable speed. Yet, before they could reach him, he felt himself being pulled from the void, the vision moving away as though the city of light was beyond his spiritual level. It was as if he had been granted a quick glimpse of a place so profound that he could only absorb a fraction of its energy. At that moment, George understood the city represented a level of existence he was not yet ready to comprehend. It was a realm of pure consciousness, love, and understanding, and though he had been shown its light, he sensed he would need further growth to truly embrace what lay within.

In an instant, George was back in the small, dim hospital room. The being of light stood beside him, glowing with the same love and calm he had felt during his journey. Looking down at the bed, George saw his own body lying still under the sheets. A strong feeling of longing filled him, and he silently begged to stay, to remain in the peaceful light rather than return. But as he held onto this wish, George felt his mind slowly being pulled back into his body.

He opened his eyes to the familiar surroundings of the hospital room and felt the weight of his body once again. Moving the sheets from his face, he realized his arms felt heavy, like lead, a stark contrast to the freedom he had just experienced. For the next three days, George drifted in and out of sleep, plagued by high fever and vivid, unsettling dreams. When he finally opened his eyes fully, he saw a nurse gazing down at him with relief. "It's good to have you back with us," she said warmly. "For a while there, we didn't think you were going to make it." She explained he had been diagnosed with double lobar pneumonia, a severe infection affecting both lungs.

As George absorbed her words, he grasped the extraordinary events that had unfolded. The day after his collapse, the ward assistant had found him unresponsive, with no detectable pulse. The doctor was called in, confirmed George's death, and instructed the assistant to prepare the body for the morgue, even pulling the sheet over George's head. Nine minutes later, as the assistant returned to transport the body, he noticed something unusual: George's hand had moved slightly. Acting on a gut feeling, he called the doctor back and suggested they try an injection of adrenaline directly into George's heart. The doctor agreed, and with the injection, a faint pulse was detected. George's life, against all odds, had been restored. Later, Dr. Donald Francy, the commanding officer, visited George personally. "Yours is the most amazing medical case I have ever encountered," he said, visibly moved by the near-miraculous turn of events.

Later in life, George held influential positions as the chairman of the Department of Psychiatry at Towers Hospital, president of the Richmond Academy of General Practice, and founder and president of the Universal Youth Corps.

Verification Events

The medical college in Richmond knew about George's recent illness and recovery and let him start the course a month late. But the pneumonia had left him weak and tired. Even though he tried hard, he couldn't keep up with the work. After only a few weeks, he failed his exams and was dropped from the program. With his training ended, George was sent back to active duty at Camp Barkeley. He traveled there by car with two other men.

As they drove into Vicksburg, Mississippi, a town George had never been to, an odd sense of familiarity overwhelmed him. The streets and landmarks felt strangely known to him, even though he was certain he had never set foot there. He predicted what was around each turn and how the shoreline would bend ahead. When the driver started to make a left turn, George urged him to go straight instead. "Just a few blocks down," he said, surprising even himself. Moments later, they pulled up in front of a white, all-night cafe with a red roof. In the right-hand window, exactly as George had seen during his NDE, stood a Pabst Blue Ribbon sign. There was the sidewalk where he had walked beside the man who couldn't see him. Across the street stood the same telephone pole, complete with the guy wire he had tried to lean on, only for his hand to pass through. The scene before him confirmed that what he had experienced at the cafe was no dream. It was the same cafe from his out-of-body experience. Somehow, what he had glimpsed in that otherworldly state was undeniably real.

George grabbed the map from the car and studied it. Tracing a straight line from Camp Barkeley to Richmond, he realized Vicksburg lay directly on that line. It was as if his out-of-body journey had somehow mirrored the very path he was now traveling in real life.

The Sphere

In December 1952, George was flipping through an issue of Life magazine when he turned a page, and his eyes locked on a drawing of a massive cutaway sphere, revealing men inside working on intricate machinery. The interior was packed with stairs, turbines, a circular tank, and a control room. It was instantly familiar. This was the same sphere he had seen during his near-death experience in 1943, in the spiritual college where beings of light were studying and working. The article explained that this sphere was a prototype engine for a new atomic submarine, a groundbreaking advancement in technology just beginning on Earth. What he had witnessed in the spiritual realm had now taken form in the physical world, eight years later.

21. The Maid, the Mother, and the Message

INGRID HONKALA

"How is this possible that you could know I was there? How could you have seen me? You were in the tank," she questioned, astonished by Ingrid's account of events she couldn't have physically witnessed.

*

Ingrid Honkala's childhood was spent in Bogotá, Colombia, where she lived with her parents and three sisters. From the start, she had health problems. Born as a very sick child, she struggled with respiratory issues, asthma, and severe allergies, which left her feeling unwell throughout the first two and a half years of her life.

At two years old, Ingrid had a Near-Death Experience when she drowned in a water tank in the back garden of her family home. That morning, Ingrid's parents left for work, leaving the children in the maid's care. Unfortunately, the maid, Maria, neglected to look after Ingrid and her four-year-old sister while their parents were away. The two young sisters entertained themselves, choosing to play catch with a ball over the water tank. "Because this tank was very big, we grabbed stools to climb onto it," Ingrid recalled. "My sister sat on the flat surface next to the tank, so she was a little safer. I went on the other side of the tank, where there was only a thin edge." Standing precariously on her side of the tank, Ingrid waited for her sister to throw the ball. Her sister tossed it, but the ball fell short and landed in the water. As Ingrid leaned forward to retrieve it, she lost her balance and fell into the tank.

People have often asked Ingrid why her sister didn't immediately call the maid for help. "We feared her because she was a lady that mistreated us," Ingrid explained. "It was something my mom didn't know." The maid's mistreatment had fostered an environment where the children felt isolated and unable to turn to her for help. As a result, they felt they had to manage situations on their own whenever their parents were away.

The water was icy and dark, and as Ingrid sank, she immediately felt her chest tighten as if it had imploded, leaving her unable to breathe. "I heard my heart pounding in my head, really, really loud," she recalled. "I went into a state of absolute horror as I realized I couldn't breathe. I was experiencing all these moments of terror." But then, something shifted. Amidst the panic, she suddenly transitioned to a state of peace and serenity. "Everything was just calm," she said. As Ingrid drifted gently through the water, she entered an all-encompassing silence where she noticed a brilliant light emanating from below, illuminating the surrounding water. "Then I started to see bubbles suspended in the water, and the bubbles were surrounded by light," she recalled. "It was like, Oh, this is amazing." Drawn by the beauty of it all, Ingrid played with the bubbles. As she turned, her gaze fell upon a body floating nearby. She recognized it instantly. It was her own. Yet, rather than feeling surprised or confused, Ingrid felt a sense of normality. It was as if seeing her own body from this perspective was entirely natural, and she accepted it without hesitation. Ingrid sensed she could return to her body if she wanted to, but the thought of re-entering a body that had been sickly for most of her life felt unappealing. Now, enveloped in an incredible sense of well-being, the idea of going back to her ailing physical form wasn't an option she wanted to consider. "So I turned around, and I left," she recalled.

As she moved away, she saw flowers blooming out of nowhere, each blossom appearing in a brilliant display around her. The flowers gently carried her from that space, surrounding her with a sense of safety and warmth. She described feeling like she was in a state similar to being in the womb, completely at peace, with nothing required of her, just pure comfort and tranquility.

Amid this sense of well-being, everything shifted in an instant, and she found herself suddenly transported to the maid's room. "Then, just like that, I am in the maid's room," Ingrid recalled. "But I'm looking at her from above, like I'm floating on the ceiling, and she's lying on her bed." From this elevated vantage point, she could see that Maria was completely unaware of what was happening to her. Ingrid observed Maria with a sense of detachment. "I just looked at her and thought, Wow, that's Maria," she remembered. The maid lay half-asleep, oblivious to the events unfolding outside in the garden. Ingrid noticed the faint sound of a soap opera playing on the radio beside her, a familiar background noise that seemed to hold the maid's sleepy attention. There was a strange sense of irony in this moment. Ingrid could observe the maid with perfect clarity, while Maria remained entirely unaware of the crisis taking place just outside.

Moments later, Ingrid was above her mother, looking down as she walked towards the bus stop. Seeing her mother was exciting, and she thought, "That's mummy." At that exact moment, her mother abruptly stopped walking, a sudden feeling washing over her that something was wrong with one of her children. Without hesitation, her mother turned and started running back toward the house. Ingrid, still in a state of peace, watched her mother with curiosity. "I'm looking at her and thinking, Oh, I wonder why she's running," she recalled.

Ingrid realized that wherever she directed her thoughts, she could go instantly. Allowing her to be anywhere simply by focusing her mind. Without warning, Ingrid found herself transported to a radiant realm of light. "This was something so incredible," she later recalled, "because there was this deep sense of going back home. For the first time in these three years of my life, I felt, wow, I am finally home." Surrounded by warmth and an overwhelming sense of welcome, Ingrid experienced a shift in her awareness and realized she was not merely Ingrid but a being of pure light.

As she settled into this place, her sense of individuality dissolved. She no longer felt confined to the identity she had known on Earth. Instead, she experienced an expansion, a feeling of being one with everything around her. Reflecting on this sensation, Ingrid described it as entering a "state of non-self," an experience of pure, formless awareness. "I experienced what I call the state of non-self over the state of nothingness," she explained. "When people ask me what nothing means, I say, the moment I try to describe what nothing means, it becomes something. So I can only tell you it is the absence of everything we know."

At the same time Ingrid was experiencing this realm of light, her mother arrived back home. Somehow, she seemed to know exactly where to go. "It was as though she had a download that gave her clarity," Ingrid explained. "She didn't go to any other room in the house, nowhere else. She went directly to the patio." Upon reaching the patio, Ingrid's mother quickly found her older daughter, who pointed to the water tank, telling her that Ingrid was inside. Without hesitation, she pulled Ingrid's small, lifeless body from the water and immediately began performing CPR. "At that moment, I was so disconnected," Ingrid recalled. "So disconnected from this body, from this reality, that I didn't feel absolutely anything. Again, in this experience, everything was happening just like a flash."

Ingrid felt herself being pulled back by a force she couldn't resist. As she re-entered her body, the familiar sensations of discomfort, pain, and confinement returned, flooding her with a sense of restriction she had not felt while she was in the realm of light. The transition was deeply jarring, and being back in her physical form was very difficult for her. "I would look at myself in the mirror and cry hysterically," she later recounted. "I would go to my mom and say, 'You don't understand, this is not me. This is not my name, and I should not be here.'" She struggled to relate to the world around her, even to other children, whom she viewed with a sense of detachment. "I would look at them and think, Oh, God, they don't know anything," she explained, feeling as though her recent experience had granted her insights that separated her from those around her.

Since her Near-Death Experience, Ingrid has maintained a connection with spiritual beings of light. This connection has become a guiding force in her life, offering her insights and wisdom beyond the ordinary. She eventually asked these beings about the reason she had her NDE, hoping to understand why she had been given such an extraordinary experience at a very young age. The beings of light told her that her NDE awakened her to a greater spiritual purpose and gave her the perspective needed to get through life differently. They explained that her role involved sharing this understanding with others, helping to bridge the gap between the physical and spiritual realms. Ingrid asked the beings of light, "Why did I waste time going to the maid's room? Why didn't I go directly to my mom?" Their response shed light on the lesson. "That's what we wanted to show you, what happens when there is no connection," they explained. The beings revealed that her detour to the maid's room was intentional, meant to show the impact of love or the lack of it. The maid had mistreated Ingrid and her siblings, creating a barrier of resentment and fear. There was no love, no genuine connection, which left the maid entirely oblivious to the crisis happening just outside.

In contrast, when Ingrid shifted her focus to her mother, the difference was immediate. Her connection with her mother was one of unconditional love, a bond so strong that it bridged the gap between the spiritual and physical realms. "Love doesn't have barriers," they said. "Whether in the spiritual world or the physical world, it doesn't matter. Love transcends everything." It was this pure, unbreakable connection that allowed her mother to sense something was wrong and rush back to the house.

Ingrid reflected on the difference in her connections. She realized that the person who was physically farthest from her, her mother, was the one who sensed her distress and ultimately came to rescue her. Her mother knew intuitively that something was wrong and returned home without hesitation. In contrast, the maid, who was only a few meters away, was completely unaware of the crisis. "Then they said when there is no connection, they will let you drown. When there is no connection, there will be division, war, and separation. So, that was just that incredible, incredible message."

Verification Events

Ingrid's Mother

When Ingrid finally shared her memories of that day with her mother, her mother listened intently, verifying that Ingrid's account was accurate. Ingrid described the details with certainty, saying, "Oh, yes, of course, that you were walking, that you were close to the bus stop, and that you ran back." Her mother was taken aback, trying to make sense of it. "How is this possible that you could know I was there? How could you have seen me? You were in the tank," she questioned, astonished by Ingrid's account of events she couldn't have physically witnessed.

Ingrid said, "I was like, Mum, I saw you."

The Maid

Years later, Ingrid researched the exact program the maid had been listening to on the radio during the time she was underwater. Driven by a desire to understand more about that pivotal moment, she discovered details about the specific soap opera playing that day, a show that had captured the maid's attention so completely that she remained oblivious to the life-threatening situation just a few meters away. This research not only provided Ingrid with factual confirmation of her memories but also highlighted the depth of her experience and the accuracy of what she had observed during her near-death experience. "I even remember the soap opera she was listening to. Later, we verified if what I was listening to was actually from the date and everything." Ingrid recalled. "I'm like, I want to verify this opera as what was playing on the radio. So that's sort of, I guess, to verify that this was really happening."

Reference

Ingrid Honkala, (2017) *'A Brightly Guided Life: How a Scientist Learned to Hear Her Inner Wisdom'*

22. Premonition and Proof: A Mother's Brush with the Beyond

STEPHANIE ARNOLD

What struck Dr. Levitt the most was that Stephanie couldn't have known these details through normal means. At the time these events occurred, Stephanie's heart had already flatlined.

*

At age 19, Stephanie Arnold visited a psychic who read the coffee stains left at the bottom of Stephanie's cup. During the session, the psychic predicted Stephanie would die at a young age. Twenty-two years later, this came true when she died giving birth to her second son.

In 2013, Stephanie was pregnant with her second child. At her 20-week ultrasound, doctors diagnosed Stephanie with placenta previa, a condition where the placenta covers the cervix. In many cases, this condition resolves on its own as the uterus grows and the placenta shifts away. If it doesn't, a C-section is typically required. However, Stephanie's intuition told her that her situation would be more serious. She worried that her placenta previa might develop into placenta accreta, a rare and dangerous condition where the placenta becomes abnormally attached to the uterine wall. This condition can lead to severe bleeding, especially during delivery. Stephanie's concern was heightened by the fact that she had a rare blood type.

As Stephanie delved deeper into researching her condition, she learned that if significant hemorrhaging occurred, an emergency hysterectomy might be necessary, and both her and the baby's lives could be at risk. "I looked at my husband, and I said, 'This is going to happen to us. The only difference is the baby is going to survive.'" Despite how alarming she must have sounded, Stephanie felt compelled to share her premonition with everyone involved in her care. "Every doctor, every nurse, any clinician who would be in my line of sight, I would tell them the same thing over and over and over again," she said.

Five months into her pregnancy, Stephanie attended a routine check-up and discovered that the placenta had not moved, confirming that a C-section would be necessary. The doctors planned her procedure for 37 weeks. Seeking advice, she talked to a friend who was a gynecological oncologist. "He said, 'Well, in the event that you need a hysterectomy during delivery, your OB wouldn't perform it; they would transfer you to maternal-fetal medicine,'" she recalled. "'But you really don't want an MFM to do it. You really want a gynecological oncologist to handle it because they have more experience with high-risk reproductive organ surgeries.'"

Stephanie had a telephone consultation with Dr. Grace Lim, an anesthesiologist, to discuss her condition and her strong sense of foreboding about the upcoming birth. She explained her concerns and her certainty that something would go wrong. Dr. Lim reassured her, saying that they were at a teaching hospital well-practiced in emergency drills and prepared for high-risk situations. Despite the reassurances, Stephanie's anxiety continued. Dr. Lim later told Stephanie, "I'll always remember the last thing you said to me, 'It is what it is.'"

During her pregnancy, Stephanie often had a craving for a cigarette. The oddity of it struck her. She didn't smoke and never had. Yet, throughout her pregnancy, this craving had been persistent and inexplicable. She found herself drawn to the scent, intentionally walking close to smokers on the street just to catch a whiff of the smoke.

At 36 weeks pregnant, Stephanie started bleeding at home. Her husband, Jonathan, rushed her to the hospital, where the seriousness of the situation became clear. The doctor decided there was no time to wait and prepared for an emergency C-section. The nurses quickly took Stephanie into the operating room. "So when they prepare you for a C-section, they put a curtain in front of your face," Stephanie explained. "Your arms are in a T. It's frigid cold. My fear is palpable because I know that the moment I deliver this baby, I'm going to die."

They performed the C-section, and Jacob, Stephanie's son, entered the world in good health. However, as soon as he was delivered, Stephanie's heart flatlined. The room exploded into urgent shouts as someone yelled, "Hit the button, call the code!" The team sprang into action while Dr Higgins called out, "It's an AFE. She's in cardiac arrest." Dr

Julie Levitt, another member of the team, appeared frozen. At this critical moment, Stephanie suffered an amniotic fluid embolism (AFE), a rare and often fatal pregnancy complication where amniotic cells enter the mother's bloodstream. If the mother is allergic to these cells, the body can go into anaphylactic shock, which is typically life-threatening.

The medical staff successfully resuscitated Stephanie after her heart had flatlined for 37 seconds. The AFE severely impaired her blood's ability to clot, leading to massive blood loss. While the human body typically holds about 20 units of blood, Stephanie required 60 units to sustain her life during the emergency.

It was unusual that there was extra blood and a crash cart already in the operating room during Stephanie's delivery. Later, she discovered that Dr. Grace Lim, the anesthesiologist, had taken her warnings seriously. Dr. Lim had never encountered a patient who spoke so confidently and insistently about a life-threatening prediction, nor one who had proactively sought specialists for her care. Deeply concerned by Stephanie's certainty, Dr. Lim had flagged her file and arranged for additional blood supplies and a crash cart to be prepared in advance.

After stabilizing Stephanie, doctors transferred her to the ICU and informed her husband that she would need a hysterectomy. She remained in a coma for six days, and when she woke up, her recovery was slow and challenging. One month later, the hospital discharged her. At first, Stephanie had no recollection of a near-death experience. "At some point, I was on a TV talk show in the States, and the host asked me, 'Did you see the light?'" Stephanie recalled. "I said, 'I don't know, man, they gave me a lot of drugs.'"

Hypnotic Regression

As time passed, Stephanie became increasingly eager to uncover what had happened during the six days she was in a coma. She couldn't shake the feeling that during those 144 hours, she might have been somewhere else.

A friend suggested she contact a hypnotherapist in Miami named Linda Burns. Stephanie felt nervous calling Linda to schedule an appointment. However, the moment she began speaking with Linda, that anxiety melted away. Linda was Jewish and from Cuba, just like Stephanie, and her slight accent reminded Stephanie of her own family. After discussing Stephanie's goals, they agreed on a date for the first meeting.

At the beginning of her regression hypnotherapy session, Stephanie set up a video camera to record the experience. Once the hypnotic induction was complete, Linda guided her back in time, and Stephanie found herself back in the operating room, viewing the scene from a third-person perspective.

"You saw in the one video of me going through the AFE, what my body was doing," she later recalled. "I was gagging. I was jerking my body. I was crying hysterically." The experience was deeply unsettling. Under hypnosis, Stephanie witnessed the medical team working to save her life. She was hovering above the scene, observing everything from a higher vantage point. Stephanie's spirit floated in front of her body, trying to communicate with the medical staff, attempting to warn them she was on the verge of dying. She could see the EKG unit on one side of her and Dr. Lim on the other.

Stephanie sensed a familiar presence. She turned and realized it was her grandmother, Ida, who had passed away 30 years ago. They drifted out of the operating room and down the hallway, drawn to the labor and delivery room where her daughters, Adina and Tessie, were playing. Tessie asked Adina to listen to a story with her, while Adina played with a blood pressure cuff, pretending to be Doc McStuffins.

In an instant, Stephanie found herself back in the operating room. She was acutely aware of her spirit's presence outside her body. As she surveyed the room, she noticed Dr Nicole Higgins, a familiar figure positioned at her feet instead of at her head, which struck her as odd. A nurse leaned in close, urging Stephanie to calm down, explaining that the stress could harm the baby.

Again, her location shifted and Stephanie found herself in a space filled with light, surrounded by other spirits. She could sense them clearly, but they felt just out of reach as if they existed on a higher level she hadn't yet reached. These spirits didn't interfere or speak, but watched her with curiosity. Although they appeared like normal people, their radiant glow made them seem ethereal. She noticed their bodies and legs but, oddly, not their feet. The setting felt like a peaceful outdoor space bathed in soft, warm light. Suddenly, Stephanie saw her Aunt Betty. She looked vibrant and youthful, as though she were in her late 30s. With a warm smile, Aunt Betty handed Stephanie a cola, something her aunt did often when she was alive. Moments later, her grandmother Rachel appeared, glowing with the same striking vitality and beauty. Her Uncle Marvin, always the supportive voice, spoke up. "I've always known you to be a fighter," he said with a grin. "You know what to do."

Stephanie floated to the maternity unit to check on her newborn son, Jacob, and saw him resting peacefully. Her awareness shifted, and she found herself in the ICU, watching Johnathan, who was sitting by her bedside, looking at her unconscious form. She hovered over his right shoulder as he whispered, "I can't live without you." She watched her brother-in-law guide her mother into the room where Johnathan was by her side.

Stephanie's uncle, Marvin, took her to her father's kitchen. She watched her father sitting at the table, tearful as he sipped an espresso. He spoke aloud, addressing her deceased uncle Marvin. "Look after her." With a touch of humor, Uncle Marvin said, "You see, even in heaven, I have to take your father's orders. I hear you, Ralph. I always hear you."

Verification Events

Dr. Julie Levitt

Stephanie later met with Dr. Julie Levitt to share a video recording of her hypnosis session. As Dr. Levitt watched the footage, the accuracy of Stephanie's detailed recollection amazed her. Every event Stephanie described matched exactly what had happened during the critical moments of her surgery. Dr. Levitt took time to clarify one point that might have seemed confusing. She explained she hadn't frozen during the operation, even though it may have appeared that way in Stephanie's memory. She also confirmed she had not performed the C-section herself, just as Stephanie had remembered during her hypnosis session. What struck Dr. Levitt the most was that Stephanie couldn't have known these details through normal means. At the time these events occurred, Stephanie's heart had already flatlined.

Her Children

Stephanie asked Tessie about her time in the labor and delivery room with Adina. Tessie confirmed Adina had indeed played with the blood pressure cuff and pretended to be Doc McStuffins, just as Stephanie had seen during her out-of-body experience. Surprised, Tessie looked at her mother and asked, "How did you know that?" The question confirmed Stephanie's memories, that what she had witnessed while unconscious was real.

VERIFIED NEAR DEATH EXPERIENCES

Dr Nicole Higgins

Stephanie played the video of her hypnotic session, where she recounted the events of Jacob's birth to Dr. Nicole Higgins. As Dr Higgins watched, her reaction was emotional and conflicted. She admitted her initial skepticism, saying, "Part of me is a little bit skeptical. The scientific part of me says that you were under anesthesia. You had no blood pressure or circulation. How could you remember this?" Despite her reservations, Dr Higgins confirmed she had indeed been standing by Stephanie's feet during the delivery, exactly as Stephanie described in her hypnotic recollection. This detail struck Dr Higgins, as Stephanie could not have seen her position in the room, especially with the surgical curtain across her neck that obscured her view. The accuracy of Stephanie's memories, considering her medical state at the time, reinforced the verification of what she had witnessed.

Uncle Marvin

Stephanie had a vivid dream about her Uncle Marvin that felt very real. She woke up believing he was in the room with her, and she noticed the scent of cigarettes lingering in the air. The craving she had experienced for cigarettes throughout her pregnancy had disappeared after the birth. She now believes that the craving had been a connection to her uncle Marvin, a reminder that he had been watching over her the whole time. It was his way of letting her know she was never alone and that he had been with her during those critical months.

Reference

Stephanie Arnold, with Sari Padorr (2015) '*37 Seconds: Dying Revealed Heaven's Help*', Harper One

23. Early 20th-Century Near-Death Experiences

The Case of W. Martin.

The following report was published in the (London) Sunday Express on May 26, 1935:

In 1911, at the age of sixteen, I was staying about twelve miles from my own home when a high wall was blown down by a sudden gust of wind as I was passing. A huge coping stone hit me on top of the head. It then seemed as if I could see myself lying on the ground, huddled up, with one corner of the stone resting on my head and quite a number of people rushing towards me. I watched them move the stone and someone took off his coat and put it under my head, and I heard all their comments: Fetch a doctor. His neck is broken. Skull smashed like an eggshell. He (apparently a doctor) then wanted to know if anyone knew where I lived, and on being told that I was lodging just around the corner he instructed them to carry me there. Now all this time it appeared as though I was disembodied from the form lying on the ground and suspended in mid-air in the center of the group, and could hear everything that was said. As they started to carry me it was remarked that it would come as a blow to my people, and I was immediately conscious of a desire to be with my mother.

Instantly, I was at home, and my father and mother were just sitting down to their midday meal. On my entrance, Mother sat bolt upright in her chair and said, Bert, something has happened to our boy. Nonsense, he said, whatever has put such an idea into your head? There followed an argument, but mother refused to be pacified, and said that if she caught the 2 p.m. train she could be with me before three and satisfy herself. She had hardly left the room when there came a knock on the front door. It was a porter from the railway station with a telegram saying I was badly hurt. Then suddenly, I was again transported. This time, it seemed to be against my wish, to a bedroom where a woman whom I recognized was in bed, two other women were quietly bustling around, and a doctor was leaning over the bed. Then the doctor had a baby in his hands. At once I became aware of an almost irresistible impulse to press my face through the back of the baby's head so that my face would come into the same place as the child's. The doctor said It looks as though we have lost them both. And again I felt the urge to take the baby's place in order to show him he was wrong, but the thought of my mother crying turned my thoughts in her direction, when straightway I was in a railway carriage with both her and father.

He (Mr. Martin's father) was looking at his watch, and she (Mr. Martin's mother) was saying that trains always crawled when you were in a hurry, and Dad's reply was that the train was right on time. I was still with them when they arrived at my lodgings and were shown into my room where I had been put to bed. Mother sat beside the bed and I longed to comfort her, and the realization came that I ought to do the same thing as I felt impelled to do in the case of the baby and climb into the body in the bed. At last, I succeeded, and the effort caused the real me to sit up in bed fully conscious. Mother made me lie down again, but I said I was all right, and remarked that it was odd she knew something was wrong before the porter had brought the telegram. Both she and Dad were amazed at my knowledge. Their astonishment further increased when I repeated almost word for word some of the conversations they had had at home and on the train. Mother remarked that she supposed that when some people came close to death, they were gifted with second sight. I replied by saying I had also been close to birth as well and told them that Mrs. Wilson, who lived close to us at home, had a baby that day. But it was dead because I would not get into its body. We subsequently learned that Mrs. Wilson died on the same day at 2:05 p.m. after delivering a stillborn girl. I am convinced that if I had willed myself into that baby's body, today I would be a Miss Wilson, instead of still being Ð W. Martin, 107 Grove Street, Liverpool.

Reference:

The Sunday Express. (1935, May 26). *(London)*.

The Ogston Case

The following was published in the book Reminiscences of Three Campaigns (1920).

The recollections of the days that followed my admission to the hospital in Bloemfontein were somewhat confusing, but my habit of making notes whenever I was able enabled me to recall some details regarding them.

I believe that unless there are such complications as perforation of the intestines, the death from typhoid is not an unpleasant one for the patient, however appalling it may appear to an onlooker. In my delirium, night and day made little difference to me. In the four-bedded ward where they first placed me, I lay, as it seemed, in a constant stupor which excluded the existence of any hopes or fears. Mind and body seemed to be dual and, to some extent, separate. I was conscious of the body as an inert tumbled mass near a door; it belonged to me, but it was not I. I was conscious that my mental self, used regularly to leave the body, always carrying something soft and black, I did not know what, in my left hand that was invariable and wander away from it under grey, sunless, moonless, and starless skies, ever onwards to a distant gleam on the horizon, solitary but not unhappy, and seeing other dark shades gliding silently by, until something produced a consciousness that the chilly mass, which I then recalled was my body, was being stirred as it lay by the door. I was then drawn rapidly back to it, joined it with disgust, and it became I, and was fed, spoken to, and cared for. When it was again left, I seemed to wander off as before, by the side of a silent, dark, slowly-flowing great flood, through silent fields of asphodel, knowing neither light nor darkness, and though I knew that death was hovering about, having no thought of religion nor dread of the end, and roamed on beneath the murky skies apathetic and contented, until something again disturbed the body where it lay, when I was drawn back to it afresh, and entered it with ever-growing repulsion. As the days went on, or rather I should say as time passed, all I knew of my sickness was that the wanderings through the dim asphodel fields became more continual and more distant, until about the end of the term of high fever I was summoned back to the huddled mass with intense loathing, and as I drew near and heard someone say ' He will live,' I remember finding the mass less cold and clammy, and ever after that the wanderings appeared to be fewer and shorter, the thing lying at the door and I grew more together, and ceased to be separated into two entities.

In my wanderings, there was a strange consciousness that I could see through the walls of the building, though I was aware that they were there and that everything was transparent to my senses. I saw plainly, for instance, a poor R.A.M.C. surgeon, of whose existence I had not known, and who was in quite another part of the hospital, grow very ill and scream and die; I saw them cover his corpse and carry him softly out on shoeless feet, quietly and surreptitiously, lest we should know that he had died, and the next night — I thought — take him away to the cemetery. Afterwards, when I told these happenings to the sisters, they informed me that all this had happened just as I had fancied. But the name of the poor fellow I never knew.

Reference:

Ogston, A. (1920). *Reminiscences of Three Campaigns*. London: Hodder & Stoughton.

The following three cases were published in the book The Phenomena of Astral Projection (1951)

The Hare Case: Haunted By a Projector?

The following case is suggestive of the fact that the wife may have haunted the dwelling in her projected dream body, which, of course, is the astral body in a semi-conscious condition.

The case is from the Revue des Etudes Psychiques (1902). The narrator (fictitiously called George P. Hare and known personally by M. César de Vesme) reported the case with a confirmatory letter from the other person concerned. Again I caution my readers not to accept this as bona fide evidence of projection of the astral body. It may not have been, but I reproduce the case as possibly involving semi-conscious (dream) projection. —S.M.)

Says Mr. Hare:

"Some time ago, my wife dreamed on several occasions of a house whose interior arrangement she was able to describe in all its details, although she had no idea where this house existed.

Later, in 1883, I leased from Lady B———, for the autumn, a house in the mountains of Scotland, surrounded by hunting lands and fishing lakes. My son, who was then in Scotland, took charge of the matter, without my wife or I ever seeing the house in question.

When I went there alone later, to sign the contract and take possession of the property, Lady B―― was still inhabiting the place. She told me that if I had no objection, she would give me a room which she herself had been occupying and which had, for some time past, been haunted by a woman who continued to appear there.

Being quite skeptical about such matters, I replied that I should be delighted to make the acquaintance of the ghost.... I went to sleep in the room, but did not see any ghost.

Later, when my wife arrived, she was astonished when she recognized the house as the one of her dreams! She went all over it; all the details corresponded with those she had so often seen in sleep. But when she went back down into the drawing-room again, she said: 'But still, this cannot be the house I saw in my dreams because there ought to be a succession of rooms that are missing here.' She was told that the rooms actually existed, but that one could not reach them through the drawing-room. When they were shown to her, she remembered each one of them clearly

She said, however, that it seemed to her that one of the bedrooms was not used for this purpose when she visited it in sleep. It was again explained to her that this room had not formerly been a bedroom, but had been changed into one.

Two or three days later, my wife and I visited Lady B. Since they were unknown to each other, I introduced them.

Lady B—— cried out in amazement: 'Why—you are the lady who has been haunting my bedroom!'"

Reference:

Muldoon, Sylvan Joseph, and Hereward Carrington (1951) *The Phenomena of Astral Projection* London: Rider

The Laufmann Case: Apparently Dead For Two Days.

For almost two days, Mr. W. A. Laufmann was apparently dead. He was staying at the time in Omaha, being a travelling salesman. He states that he was conscious of something like a fleecy ball releasing itself from his physical form. When exteriorized, the 'fleecy ball' expanded into the shape of a man, but a man almost three feet taller than his physical form!

"It was standing there in the middle of the room," says Mr. Laufmann, "'and distinctly saw my dead body lying upon the bed. . .. I started to leave the room and met one of the physicians and was surprised that he said nothing to me, but since he made no effort to stop me, I walked out into the street where I met an acquaintance of mine, Mr. Milton Blose.

I tried to greet Mr. Blose by hitting him on the back, but my arm went through him. . .. It was impossible for me to attract his attention. . .. I saw that he went across the street and looked into a shop window where a miniature 'Ferris wheel' was on display."

Returning to the hospital, Mr. Laufmann went through the door of the room where his physical self lay, and there he saw the doctors standing over his corpse discussing the case.

"One of the doctors tried the experiment of applying an electric current to my feet, and although I was standing outside my physical body, in the center of the room, I felt it (the electric current) with intense agony . . . and I knew momentarily that I was back in my body again."

Mr. Laufmann claimed to possess a testimonial letter from Mr. Blose verifying the fact that the latter actually had been in Omaha at the time and had walked down the street and stopped to look at a 'Ferris wheel' in a shop window.

Reference:

Muldoon, Sylvan Joseph, and Hereward Carrington (1951) *The Phenomena of Astral Projection* London: Rider

The Swoboda Case: Hurled Into Her Physical Body

This is one of several experiences related to Fraulein Sophie Swoboda, which I have translated from German. One day, Sophie had a violent headache and, lying down on the sofa, fell fast asleep. While in the sleep state, she became awake and noticed that her mother was quietly leaving the room; in fact, it was the mother's leaving that seemed to awaken her.

Sophie noticed that she no longer had the headache, and that she was feeling quite light. . .. Arising from the sofa, she followed her mother to tell her of the improvement in her condition. Reaching her mother—who was now sitting, knitting, beside her father, who was reading aloud—Sophie observed that they did not see her.

She stood there beside her mother and father quite unnoticed, although she could see everything that they were doing. After a time, her mother set aside her knitting, arose, and went back into the room where the sofa stood, being somewhat anxious about her daughter's condition.

Although Sophie tried, she could not make herself perceptible to her mother. . .. Then she saw herself lying on the sofa. Her eyes were closed, and she was pale and corpse-like.

In another moment, Sophie felt herself actually thrown back upon the sofa into her physical body. She said it was as if she had been thrown or hurled back with a blow. It was with great effort that she was able to open her eyes.

She tells how she amazed her parents by repeating word for word the very text that her father had been reading and giving them an accurate account of their conversation—although physically she had been asleep—three rooms away, with the doors between them closed.

In another place, Fraulein Swoboda tells of being exteriorized from her physical self and of being seen by a percipient who observed not only the inert material body but the projected double at the same time.

The account states that Fraulein Swoboda was sitting on a sofa beside a friend, Frau B——. They were listening to Irma (Frau B——'s daughter) playing the piano, which was on the opposite side of the room. As Fraulein Swaboda leaned back and closed her eyes, she had the experience of crossing the room and standing beside Irma at the piano. She noticed that the hostess, Frau B——, was looking at her in amazement. . ... Then, to her own amazement, Fraulein Swoboda saw that her own physical self was still sitting on the sofa with closed eyes. ... While standing there, Fraulein Swoboda noticed that Frau B—— kept looking first at the body beside her on the sofa, then at the double standing at the piano, as if in great bewilderment.

Fraulein Swoboda hurried back to her physical self, and as her eyes opened, she began to tell of her experience, which was verified by Frau B——, who told her how she had seen both Fraulein Swoboda's bodies simultaneously—the one upon the sofa and the one standing beside the piano.

Reference:

Muldoon, Sylvan Joseph, and Hereward Carrington (1951) *The Phenomena of Astral Projection* London: Rider

24. Dr. Rudy's Christmas Day Case

I have been lucky to get permission to add this report from The International Association for Near-Death Studies Journal of Near-Death Studies.

A Near-Death Experience with Veridical Perception Described by a Famous Heart Surgeon and Confirmed by his Assistant Surgeon

From The International Association for Near-Death Studies Journal of Near-Death Studies, Vol. 31 Titus Rivas, M.A., M.Sc. Rudolf H. Smit

On July 27, 2011, Mike Milligan, DMD (http://www.eastland dental.com/) uploaded a fascinating video clip onto his YouTube account, dentalmastermind, entitled Famous Cardiac Surgeon's Stories of Near-Death Experiences in Surgery (http://www.youtube.com/watch?v=JL1oDuvQR08). It concerns a segment taken from a larger interview Milligan had conducted with the late U.S. cardiac surgeon Lloyd William Rudy, Jr., M.D. (1934–2012) during a meeting of the American Academy for Oral Systemic Health (AAOSH). In June 2011, Rudy graduated from the University of Washington Medical School, completed a residency at the University of San Francisco Medical Centre, and, after serving in a M.A.S.H. unit in Vietnam, became a Board Certified Cardiovascular and Thoracic Surgeon, was Dean of the Heart Program at the University of Georgia

School of Medicine, and was a member of the first heart transplant team at Stanford University. The Governor of Montana proclaimed a Dr. Lloyd Rudy Day in honor of his pioneering work in cardiac surgery in that state. In the YouTube clip, Rudy discussed two cases he had witnessed, the first of which concerned a classic NDE involving veridical perception during clinical death. Following is a transcript of this portion of the interview:

RUDY: We had a very unfortunate individual who, on Christmas Day, had, from an oral infection, infected his native valve (gestures to indicate a valve of the heart, with "native" referring to the patient's biological valve rather than an artificial, prosthetic valve). If your native valve has the slightest defect, whether you were born with it or you developed it later— it calcified a little, and the valve leaflets don't move or whatever— the body recognizes that as something abnormal that it's got to take care of. So that's what happened to this man, and one of my junior partners was on call, and he had to do an emergency valve resection. Once we were able to accomplish the repair of the aneurysm and the replacement of the valve, we could not get the person off of the bypass. Every time the four or five liters of blood that we were pumping around his body, we would reduce down to two or three, he'd begin to weaken, and his blood pressure would go down, and so on.

To make a long story short, we simply couldn't get him off the heart-lung machine. Finally, we just had to give up. I mean, we said: We cannot get him off of the heart-lung machine, so we're going to have to pronounce him dead. So, we did that. And so the anesthesiologist turned his machine off, and the bellows that were breathing for the patient stopped. That machine was quiet. The anesthesiologist went into the surgeon's lounge. He hadn't eaten anything all day, so he went in to have a sandwich. Then the people, who usually clean up the instruments and all that, were coming in and taking away all these tools. And my surgical assistant closed the patient in a way that a postmortem exam could be done because anyone who succumbs on the table by law has to have an autopsy. So he closed him up briefly, with a couple or three wires here and a big stitch to close his soft tissue. Well, that machine that records the blood pressure, and the pulse, and the left atrial pressure, and all the monitoring lines and things continued to run the paper out onto the floor in a big heap. Nobody bothered to turn it off. And then we put down a trans-esophageal echo-probe, which is just a long tube that has a microphone on the end of it, and we can get a beautiful picture on a monitor of the heart beating.

Well, that machine was left on, and the VCR tape continued to run. Well, the assistant surgeon and I went in and took our gowns off, and gloves and masks and things, and came back, and we were in our short-sleeve shirts, and we were standing at the door, kind of discussing if there was anything else we could have done and any other medicines we could have given, whatever, to have made this a success. And as we were standing there, it had been at least 20 minutes. I don't know this exact time sequence, but it was close to 20–

25 minutes that this man recorded no heartbeat, no blood pressure (gestures to indicate the monitoring machine's continuous paper readout), and the echo showing no movement of the heart, just sitting.

And all of a sudden, we looked up, and this surgical assistant had just finished closing him, and we saw some electrical activity. And pretty soon, the electrical activity turned into a heartbeat. Very slow, 30, 40-a-minute, and we thought, "Well, that's kind of an agonal thing," and we see that, occasionally, the heart will continue to beat even though the patient can't generate a blood pressure or pump any blood. Well, pretty soon we look, and he's actually generating a pressure. Now, we are not doing anything; I mean, the machines are all shut off. And we'd stopped all the medicines and all that. So I started yelling, "Get anesthesia back in here!" and, "Get the nurses!" To make a very long story short, without putting him back on cardiopulmonary bypass or heart-lung machine and stuff, we started giving him some medicines, and anesthesia started giving him oxygen. And pretty soon, he had a blood pressure of 80, and pretty soon a blood pressure of 100, and his heart rate was now up to 100 a minute. He recovered and had no neurologic deficit.

And for the next 10 days (to) two weeks, all of us went in and were talking to him about what he experienced, if anything. And he talked about the bright light at the end of the tunnel, as I recall, and so on. But the thing that astounded me was that he described that operating room floating around and saying, "I saw you and Dr. Cattaneo standing in the doorway with your arms folded, talking. I saw the – I didn't know where the anesthesiologist was, but he came running back in. And I saw all of these Post-its (Post-it® notes) sitting on this TV screen. And what those were, were any call I got, the nurse would write down who called and the phone number and stick it on the monitor, and then the next Post-it would stick to that Post-it, and then I'd have a string of Post-its of phone calls I had to make. He described that. I mean, there is no way he could have described that before the operation because I didn't have any calls, right?

MILLIGAN: And he's sitting, he's lying on the (gestures to indicate surgical table) – so he must have been floating?

RUDY: He was up there. He described the scene, things that there is no way he knew. I mean, he didn't wake up in the operating room and see all this. (Milligan: No.) I mean, he was out (Milligan: Right) and was out for, I don't know, even a day or two while we recovered him in the intensive care unit. So, what does that tell you? Was that his soul up there?

MILLIGAN: It's hard to know, but it certainly brings that possibility into play.

RUDY: It always makes me very emotional.

After Milligan uploaded this video clip onto YouTube in October 2011, psychiatrist and NDE researcher Bruce Greyson brought the interview to the attention of researcher Jan Holden suggested that she, as Editor of this Journal, send Rudy a letter inviting him to submit the case for publication as a case study; and gave her Rudy's address. She received no reply, and in subsequent correspondence with researcher Chris Carter, she learned that Rudy had died in April 2012. Simultaneously, the case had aroused our own interest, and co-author Titus Rivas had also tried to reach Rudy by email. In the meantime, Milligan's entire interview with Rudy was up loaded onto the AAOSH website (http://aaoshconnect.org/issue/ march-20122013/article/aaosh- video- interviews). For this reason, co-author Rivas approached Milligan to ask him for more details. Milligan sent the following reply:

I met Dr. Rudy during an AAOSH meeting in Chicago in June 2011 and had dinner with him where he told me about these experiences. I asked him to video them as I felt many people would be interested – I told him very few people would have the perspective he had, being a cardiac surgeon, etc. He reluctantly agreed, and we did the videos the next day. He was a wonderful and gracious man and a pleasure to be with. Sadly, Dr. Rudy has passed away since we did the videos. (M. Milligan, personal communication, November 8, 2012)

Milligan also suggested two people who might have more information about the case, but when Rivas contacted them, unfortunately, they did not. In January 2013, a correspondent from the UK alerted co-author Smit to an online comment Roberto Amado-Cattaneo, M.D., had made to Milligan's YouTube clip. Amado-Cattaneo was the physician Rudy had referred to in his interview as his assistant cardiac surgeon, "Dr. Cattaneo." At the time of his comment, Amado-Cattaneo was connected to CardioWest Cardiothoracic

Surgery in Great Falls, Montana. The comment, dated January 23, 2013, was:

Everything that Dr. Lloyd Rudy explained in this video is absolutely true. I was there with him doing this surgery. The patient fully recovered, and what he said to us after the surgery is what he experienced. – Dr. Roberto Amado-Cattaneo, cardiac surgeon, Great Falls, Montana.

On January 28, 2013, co-author Titus Rivas contacted Amado-Cattaneo by email, and Amado-Cattaneo agreed to answer a few questions, also by email. Here are his replies:

This case happened sometime late 1990's early 2000's. I do not know the patient's identity anymore. Neither do I think we can find out, unfortunately. It has been too long, and I do not have any records of that case anymore. My role was that of assistant surgeon. I was in the case from beginning to end. I did witness the entire case and everything that my partner Dr. Rudy explained in the video. I do not have a rational scientific explanation to explain this phenomenon. I do know that this happened. This patient had close to 20 minutes or more of no life, no physiologic life, no heartbeat, no blood pressure, no respiratory function whatsoever, and then he came back to life and told us what you heard on the video.

He recovered fully. I do not think there was something wrong with the monitoring devices. The reason is that there are different types of monitors, and they were left on. We could see a flatline, the monitor was on but not recording electrical activity in the heart. When he started coming back, we could see at first a slow beat that eventually evolved into something real closer to normal. The same with the ultrasound scan placed inside the esophagus; we saw no heart activity for the 20 minutes or so, machine still on, and then it started showing muscle movement, that is, contractility of the heart muscle that eventually turned into close to normal function, able to generate a blood pressure and life.

The reason we saw him coming back is that fact that the monitors were on, and so we saw him regaining life; when this happened, we restarted full support with drugs, oxygen, etc. This was not a hoax; no way, this was as real as it gets. We were absolutely shocked that he would come back after 20 or more minutes, we had pronounced him dead on the operating room table and told the wife that he had died. I have seen people recover from profound and prolonged shock, but still having life; in this case there was no life. (R. Amado-Cattaneo, personal communication, January 28 and 30, 2013).

Subsequently, Rivas sent Amado-Cattaneo several additional questions suggested to him by Jan Holden and Bruce Greyson about the veracity and normal explicability of the patient's statements and about the location of the monitor with Post-it messages, respectively. Amado-Cattaneo replied as follows:

I do not believe he said anything that we questioned as being real, we thought all along his description was quite accurate regarding things he said he saw or heard. Patients' eyes are always shut during surgery; most of the time, they are taped so they do not open since this can cause injury to the corneas. (R. Amado- Cattaneo, personal communication, February 13th, 2013).

There are many non-sterile equipment in an operating room including monitors. Monitors are close range so surgeons can "monitor different parameters through the case." The messages to Dr. Rudy, I believe, were taped to a monitor that sits close to the end of the operating table, up in the air, close enough for anybody to see what it is there, like the patient, for example, if he was looking at it. (R. Amado-Cattaneo, personal communication, February 15th, 2013).

Our UK correspondent also had contacted Amado-Cattaneo who told him the incident took place at the Deaconess Hospital in Spokane, Washington. Amado-Cattaneo's testimony is very valuable, as it explicitly confirms Rudy's account. The evidential value of this case is increased because of the component of the Post-it notes, which involved seemingly out-of-body visual perception of phenomena during documented continuous eyes-closed unconsciousness that was highly unlikely to have been deduced from sensory input such as hearing or from logical deduction. Neither Rudy nor Cattaneo indicated that the patient reported any erroneous content.

This case appears to belong to those most evidential cases of AVP in which perceptions during an NDE were confirmed as completely accurate by objective observers. We believe that the accumulation of such anecdotal evidence is making it increasingly difficult to dismiss this type of case out of hand. Of course, this case would be complete if the identity of the patient could be established so that medical records could be examined, but unless Amado-Cattaneo recalls his name, such further investigation is not feasible. However, in our view, this imperfection only slightly reduces, but in no way negates, the case as serious evidence for AVP.

References:

Holden, J. M. (2009). Veridical perception in near-death experiences. In J. M. Holden, B. Greyson, & D. James (Eds.), *The handbook of near-death experiences: Thirty years of investigation* (pp. 185–212). Santa Barbara, CA: Praeger/ABC-CLIO.

Rivas, T., & Dirven, A. (2010). *Van en naar het licht [From and to the light]*. Leeuwarden, The Netherlands: Elikser.

Smit, R. H. (2008). Corroboration of the dentures anecdote involving veridical perception in a near-death experience. *Journal of Near-Death Studies, 27*(1), 47–61. https://doi.org/10.17514/JNDS-2008-27-1-47-61

The production of this book was finished in March 2025

Produced by:

Grapevine Books
ajparrbooks@gmail.com

FIRST EDITION
LONDON 2025
Copyright © 2025 Simon Bown

Made in the USA
Monee, IL
30 March 2025